At Home

Blessings

Lucy

By

Lucy Holt

At Home with God

Author: Lucy Holt

Copyright © Lucy Holt (2022)

The right of Lucy Holt to be identified as author of this work has been asserted by the author in accordance with section 77 and 78 of the Copyright, Designs and Patents Act 1988.

First Published in 2022

ISBN 978-1-915492-55-5 (Paperback)

Book cover design and Book layout by:
Maple Publishers
www.maplepublishers.com

Front Cover Image Credit:
'Joy'
Bronze on Clipsham limestone
by Ali Hutchison
(@alihutchisonart)

Published by:
Maple Publishers
1 Brunel Way,
Slough,
SL1 1FQ, UK
www.maplepublishers.com

For Brian John, my Dear Old Dad, who taught me so much about love and faith, and with confidence I can say he is now truly At Home with God. With much love.

CONTENTS

Home is.... Belonging, Retreat, Heartbeat

Anne-Marie, Dorset

Introduction

In 2020 with the start of the global pandemic we were told clearly to "Stay at Home" and "Work from home where possible". During the last few years perhaps our homes, at times, have felt both claustrophobic and we really wanted to get out, but also a refuge and a place of safety in the middle of what felt an unsure and unsafe world. So why write a book about Home?

This book says things I would have loved to be able to say to people personally but, perhaps, haven't been brave enough to – so I write it instead! It has come out of a very difficult few years and a time when I have experienced grief and difficulty in the same way many others have too. From the start, I want to say this is a personal book about my journey with God and how this has formed me and made me the person I am today.

A few days ago, a little girl came to my door with Sue, a friend of her grandmother. After meeting my husband and leaving him with some beautiful plants for me, she turned to Sue and said: "I like that home; it smells like lasagne; it's a happy home." I was deeply touched because this little girl had picked up a vibe about my home. It didn't literally smell of lasagne, but in her mind, it represented the smell of lasagne; something she enjoyed eating and something that she and her family would sit and eat together. She used the description of a smell to describe the vibe she got from my home. A place where she would be welcome, where she could enjoy being in the house and sharing with those within it.

For many people, however, the experience of home has not been happy for a variety of reasons. Home contains relationships, and relationships can be tricky. We all get things wrong, and our own experience of life can lead us to react in different ways to others. For some, home may have been a place of deep pain, leaving emotions they are still trying to work through. It is really important to recognise this here. I seriously do not want to deny this experience for so many people as we look at the concept of home in this book. I hope and pray that as this book is read we may all recognise places where we have felt at home and where the concept of home has had real meaning.

I hope also that you won't stop reading because you think that I'm going to talk about my perfect experience of home, either while growing up or now. Although I have generally had a happy experience of home, those who have lived with me would say that things weren't always perfect. After all, I'm only human, and I don't always react in the way I would if I had the wisdom of hindsight. I have been parented by some special parents and I have parented my own children, but I know that even within these relationships we have slipped up and made mistakes. I remember my sister getting something wrong when my nephew was very little. She told him that she was sorry but sometimes Mummies don't always get things right. To which the quick reply of a bright young thing came back: "Well Mummy you will just have to try harder."

This book explores how the concept of "At Home with God" can transform the inadequacies of our earthly homes and suggests that there can be so much more to our lives as we live out a new relationship with Him.

I have for most of my life, as well as reading novels (and I do love a murder mystery) read Christian literature. I have read a mound of books that tell me what I should do to become a Christian, what steps I need to take and how this is going to change my life. However, I've never been a fan of the tick-box list to salvation; acknowledgement of sin, asking for forgiveness and praying a prayer. It would be wrong to say that these things are not important, but most of us don't go through a linear process with faith. We move backwards and forwards; we pray and we doubt, God seems present; then He seems to have disappeared. If I was to say when I became a Christian I would have to describe not one event when it all made sense but a development of thought and realisation, and a growing sense of God's grace and majesty, I would say: "it's been a journey for me", and it continues to be as I meander through life and try to work out my faith in the midst of it all

The Apostle Paul is well known for his Damascus Road experience. He had an awesome encounter with Jesus and was a changed man from that day forward. But in his prolific writing, we see evidence of his growth as a Christian even beyond his dramatic conversion. Even Paul had to work out what that meant for his life and he helped others do the same. Perhaps, because of Paul's personality, encountering Jesus in this way was the only way that God was going to get through to this hard-headed man. Most people don't have such radical conversion experiences, but their faith grows gradually as they develop a relationship with God.

The Christian faith is not just a transaction; it's a relationship with God. In any relationship there can be moments of transaction: "If I do this then you'll do that...", but most of the time we just get on with getting to know each other, supporting and showing each other how much we mean to each other. If our relationships with those we love are based on the expectation of "what I will get out of it if I put this in", in other words primarily transactional, they would be really hard to sustain and ultimately not rewarding. The beauty of the Christian faith is that it's not transactional, but all about a two-way relationship that is safe and brings us back spiritually to where we belong.

Where we belong is our home, and as I pondered this I was struck by these words from Psalm 90:

*God, it seems you've been **our home forever**; long before the mountains were born, long before you brought earth itself to birth, from "once upon a time" to "kingdom come"—you are God.* [1]

Pondering this theme of "God as our home forever", I began to realise that home is the basis for so many important relationships that we have. As I reflect on what has happened in my own life, I realise how important having a space of safety despite any difficulties is, and this makes so much sense as a way of understanding my relationship with God that I hope, in this book, to explore and share these thoughts with you.

In June 2021, I was deeply privileged to be present when my own Father left this life to go to his Heavenly home, having come back to his earthly home from hospital for a short period of time. The concept of Home here was so important as we experienced what I can only describe as a thin-place between earth and heaven that evening. And part of my faith is the hope of eternity that Jesus spoke of when he said that his Heavenly Father had prepared a room for us in His home [2]

All these things led to the writing of these words, which I dedicate to my dear old Dad, who taught me so much about

---

[1]   *Psalm 90:1-2 The Message*

[2]   "Do not let your hearts be troubled. You believe in God[a]; believe also in me. 2 My Father's house has many rooms; if that were not so, would I have told you that I am going there to prepare a place for you? 3 And if I go and prepare a place for you, I will come back and take you to be with me that you also may be where I am. 4 You know the way to the place where I am going." John 14:1-4 NIV

not only living at home with myself, but also dwelling At Home with God.

I hope that you will find some of these words helpful to begin to explore this concept for yourself. I will give some ideas for reflection at the end of each chapter to allow you to explore the themes a little more if you would like to. But above all, I hope that you will find in my words something of the amazing way a relationship with God can truly be our Home.

Introduction ideas for reflection:

What words would you use to describe your experience of Home?

If my home smelt like lasagne- what would your happy home smell like and why?

A house is where you live a home is where you can be

Darren, Dorset

Chapter 1

What is Home?

I sit in a chair, in a room which contains a plethora of stuff that helps me realise I am both at home, and that home is a place for me for both work and family life. The room contains memories held in picture frames, or in the titles of books, and in the little wooden statues bought in an olive wood shop in Bethlehem. The books on the shelf remind me not only of the work I do, but also of the things that interest me; recipe books, books on travel, or the murder mystery I can't recycle to the charity shop as there may be a chance, I'll want to read it again. This is one room in my home and yet this room contains so much about me. The home I live in is littered with such rooms, each perhaps saying something slightly different about the things that are important to us as a family, or about the people who we have shared this home with.

The question of what home is and how we know that we are at home is one which is not easy to answer. Home seems to be a very multi-faceted interaction of place and emotion, of physicality and psychology. Home is much more than simply where I live but is a deeply emotional reaction to place. I remember a wonderful lady who had lived in her house in our town for over 30 years, and yet still spoke of going home when she made a return visit to the Welsh valleys of her childhood. So, what is it that makes somewhere a home? And then how do I know when I am at home? What is it that I feel, or what emotions does that feeling evoke?

I grew up in the leafy suburbs of Surrey and yet moved from this area as a young adult when I started training in London and my parents sold our family home and moved away. In the process of my parents moving, I lost the sense of this area being my home and I never really considered staying with them in later life as going home. I am also unusual in that I have moved around more than is normal in my adult life and lived in houses that come with my professional role, so they are never truly your own. The home I live in will not be my forever home, nor do I own it, so in many ways it feels quite temporary, and yet it is home for now. So why is that? Is it to do with what is within my home, the memories contained within all the stuff? I am sure also that moving regularly has made me very adept at making a house a home quickly. I have learnt to hang up pictures and to unpack most things quickly rather than prevaricating about the very best place for our belongings. In this way the home is established ready for my work life to begin and family life to continue.

But despite this not being my forever home, driving up the estuary, smelling the sea and listening to the squawk of gulls makes me realise I am on my way home. These are physical things in life that remind us of where we belong. I remember a distinct time, having moved to just outside Windsor to become a Vicar, when I realised that where I lived had become my home. I was driving over Dorney common and saw the Royal Standard flying over Windsor Castle, and at this point I realised that, not only was the Queen in her home, but I was on the way to mine, this was now home. A friend living in Southeast USA says she knows she is at home when she hears the sound of the cicadas and crickets at night. There are so many things we associate with home and when we are away from these things the memory of them can lead us to be homesick.

The psychological concept of home is one which is much more difficult to quantify and describe than the physical concept. As my Welsh lady demonstrated it is possible to live in a house and yet feel at home somewhere entirely different. Feeling at home may have nothing to do with the physical space that you are in and much more to do with the emotions that you feel. For many people the physical space they inhabit may not be a place of nurture or love. Many people grow up, and indeed continue to live, in homes where there is little love, acceptance or welcome. Perhaps for them the psychological sense of home may be found in a completely different place where they experience love and acceptance. This could be in the home of a friend or member of their family, perhaps even a school, therapy service or community group.

The concepts of home as a place of love, acceptance and welcome speak to us as humans at a very deep level. Psychologically they are things that we need to experience to be fully human and interact with others. And yet these are things that we primarily develop during our times at home and our interactions with those we love.

For a small piece of research, I asked some of my friends to share the words that they associate with home. You will see some of these comments as quotes at the start of each chapter. The results were not entirely surprising but fell into several distinct categories. They were predominantly associated with our inner selves and psychological wellbeing rather than merely a distinct place and some of them I have recorded here under headings:

Home as a place of Safety:

- Haven

- Sanctuary
- Emotional safety and wellbeing
- Home is where I can be myself, say and wear what I want without judgement. Home is where I can love and be loved, where I can choose who I will or won't see.
- Safe harbour place of peace and love

Home as a place of Belonging:

- Where the people I love belong
- Family
- A place to laugh, to be silly without feeling embarrassed, and to share food, drink, thoughts, ideas, hopes and dreams with the family.
- Where you are known accepted and loved

Home as a place of Being:

- Like a big hug, comfort
- Retreat, heartbeat
- Shoes off, cat on lap, hot tea, hugs, giggles, adventure planning (and endless piles of washing!)
- A house is where you live . A home is where you can "be".

I am so grateful for these insights and others from friends far and wide. They speak very clearly of the amazing way that home helps us to develop, grow and thrive as human beings. But on thinking of these concepts, I also realise how strongly they describe my relationship with God. I can see there are huge resonances between our growth as humans at home and our growth as spiritual beings. I can notice that the emotions that we experience when we feel truly at home of love, care, safety, belonging and support, can also be seen clearly in how God relates to us. Alongside this I can identify that the way that we live out our home lives can reflect the ways we can live out our faith and grow in a relationship with God.

In the Old Testament of the Bible, in the times before Jesus, the concept of home and homeland had deep significance. For the people of Israel their physical location was associated with both God's promise to them, and His presence with them. So, we see in the book of Exodus God leading the Israelites into a new home as they make the journey from Exodus and slavery in Egypt, into the promised land. The promised land was where their home was to be as God's people. And yet in the story of the Israelites we see them removed, time and time again, from their home by other nations and having to spend time in exile. Yet, in exile they do not forget their home, as we see in these words from Psalm 137:

> By the rivers of Babylon we sat and wept
> when we remembered Zion.
>
> [4] How can we sing the songs of the Lord
> while in a foreign land?
> [5] If I forget you, Jerusalem,
> may my right hand forget its skill.[3]

For the Israelites, their physical home and homeland was of such importance that within their captivity it was a place that they longed to return too. Time and time again they were to hear the promise of God through the prophets that this would be the case. The Israelites linked their physical home with their relationship with God. Yet, their physical home had a huge importance to them for their national identity.

---

[3]   Psalm 137:1, 4-5 NIV

With the New Testament things begin to change and move outwards from just the Israelite nation. The start of the stories about Jesus contains a puzzling visit to the baby by wise men from the East. This is just a hint that Jesus may just be about to turn the assumption that the God of Israel was just for the Israelites upside down.

But also, we see with Jesus the importance of home as a place of encounter. When Jesus spends time with others, He does so often in their own homes, and not in religious places such as the synagogue. Repeatedly we see Him visiting people, having meals with them and spending time in their homes. During these times we see Him teach and bring healing to those brought to Him. Why did He do this? I wonder if this has a great deal to say about how God wants to interact with us in our everyday lives. If God made us as spiritual beings, then He wants us to experience this part of our lives all the time not just in a special place or at a specific event.

So, it is possible to see the development of "At Home with God" throughout the Bible. When we are "At Home with God" we are not just in a physical space as were the Israelites in their promised land, but we are in a spiritual and psychological reality. We can be "At Home with God" in our own homes, in the homes of others or even down the pub as well as in Church! And the invitation from God is to allow Him to be at home with us and to make our home with Him as we shall see later.

Questions to ponder:

What physical things give you a sense of coming home?

If Jesus came to your home what sort of conversation might you have with him?

Home is where you are known, accepted and loved

Simon, Dorset

Chapter 2

Home is where I am truly known.

As we have begun to see, the concept of home contains a multitude of meanings. Developing a sense of "being" in our homes seems to be key. I am pretty certain though, that there is a strong link between this, and being truly known as we are. So, let's begin our exploration here.

The other day, in the middle of nowhere, I woke up in my caravan at 4.30 to the sound of the dawn chorus. It was a beautiful sound – until I realised the time. However, as I listened, and also tried to get back to sleep, I was struck by how beautiful each individual song was. I wondered which birds were making which tweet, and I even thought for a moment I might download an app on my phone to find out.

Just as the individual noises of birds can merge into one beautiful dawn chorus, the individuals are lost within the whole, so the individual beauty of humanity can be lost in the same way. If you go into a tube station at rush hour in normal times you will see a huge representation of humanity and unless someone really stands out, for their appearance or behaviour, mostly the picture we have merges into one. Trying to find the individual can be like trying to do a huge version of the famous game "Where's Wally"! And yet in terms of our identity we know that the individual is so important.

The value of each of our individuality is a key issue seen in schools, with the onus on developing self-esteem. We try hard to build up each child to value themselves and to see areas of their lives where they are different as positive traits. Low self-esteem, we know, can have a detrimental effect on mental health throughout life. But at the heart of self-esteem is the onus that the individual is just that, an individual with their own gifts, abilities, idiosyncrasies and humour.

Accepting our own individual specialness is not always easy. The concept of who we are can be hugely influenced not only by what we think about ourselves, but what we think others think about us. Often our own perceptions of ourselves can be completely different to the perceptions of others. Quite a few years ago I went on an assertiveness course with a dear friend. People laughed when we told them we were doing this course as they saw us already as two very assertive people. In contrast to their perceptions we had entered the course to boost our own self-assertiveness which we thought was lacking. To this day I am not sure who's perceptions were right!

Then on top of our perceptions of how we are seen, our individual sense of self is often flawed in the way we compare ourselves with others. I am sure I am not alone in falling into this trap of comparison. Whether as a child in how I performed at school, or on the netball pitch, and then the figure or the face, compared with the supposed concepts of beauty portrayed in magazines and on our screens. Comparing ourselves with others is not something that necessarily goes away as we grow up.

In my life comparing myself with others has led to rather an unfortunate streak of competitiveness. I think this comes partly from being the youngest child in the family, and partly from feeling somehow a need to show that I am as good as others. I vividly remember a group exercise on a clergy training course. I happened to be in a group with the most competitive men on the course and together we were a force to be reckoned with. The task was about acquiring resources and each team could go all out to succeed for themselves or work more collaboratively with the other groups. Of course, we pulled out all the stops to demolish the other groups only to find that we were left high and dry because the way the task was put together meant that real success came from working collaboratively. It was a tough lesson for us all as young vicars to come to terms with, and all of us were quite embarrassed by just how our competitiveness had caught us out and showed in a not too attractive light. Although in some ways my competitiveness has led me to strive to do things and succeed, it has also led me into difficult relationships with others and, as in the case of this exercise, left me not very proud of my actions.

How others see us and our perceptions of ourselves can also be played out in the way we dress and act. To this day, if I am going to have to deal with a difficult situation, I dress for the occasion. I will make a special effort to ensure that I look like the person I am trying to portray; in other words a dog collar and jacket with smart skirt or trousers. If I am going to a more relaxed meeting, then the cardigan will come out. How we dress can help us to feel confident in the roles we are expected to play, and that others will see us in certain ways.

All these factors point to the fact that often our perceptions and the perceptions of others do not fully reflect us as individuals. In different situations we will dress and behave to show a different part of our character. Down the centuries this has been written about in the way of wearing a mask to show different facets of our character. But who are we truly, and who knows us as we truly are?

So what has all this got to do with our question of how we are "At Home with God?". I would hazard a guess that for most of us the place of home is one where we can truly be ourselves and be genuinely known for who we are. If our home is a comfortable and a good place, then generally, those we live with accept us as we are and for who we are. We can often let the barriers down, remove the masks, wear our PJs, and relax as who we are. This is the concept I want to explore here. This sense of being truly who we are at Home and being truly who we were meant to be "At Home with God".

A lot of people when they hear that I am a vicar, say, "I'm not religious but I am a spiritual person". One of the most spiritual experiences I have encountered is swimming with a group of sea bathers as the sun rises at dawn in the English Channel. Many of us are moved by a beautiful sunset or awed by a powerful thunderstorm. These can be spiritual moments and can lead us to marvel and wonder

For me being a spiritual person is part of life, a natural way we express ourselves and sometimes surprising in the intensity of feelings it brings. Back some 1600 years ago, St Augustine wrote these words, which seem still very relevant today.

"Thou hast made us for thyself, O Lord, and our heart is restless until it finds its rest in thee."[4]

In these simple words he describes that part of our life that surprises us with that emotion. But I think it is also describing that part of our life that often asks the question "is this what it's all about, is my life just this, or is there something more?" I have heard this yearning described in other ways as the God shaped hole within us, so why is it there? Why are our hearts restless as Augustine described?

---

4   Augustine of Hippo, Confessions

And this goes back to why God created us in the first place. The stories of creation in the Bible, whether read literally or figuratively, speak to us of an intense relationship between God and humankind. We are told in Genesis 1:27:

"So God created mankind in his own image, In the image of God he created them; male and female he created them."

If He created humankind in His image there is something of God within each one of us. The spiritual side of our lives is important, and God created us in His image for this. The first man and woman wandered around the garden together at ease with each other. That picture tells us that God created humankind for His delight, in His image to be in relationship with Him. But the biblical story continues with the account of humankind getting it disastrously wrong and no longer being in relationship with God. And yet as we will later explore, this close relationship with Him is his deepest desire for us.

The words of Psalm 139 speak so powerfully about God's creation of us. In my experience of working with parents and young babies, in my previous career as a Health Visitor, I never failed to wonder at the miracle of creation. I never failed to be awed by the amazing way that babies are so perfect, and such a sense of expectation of what they are to become. In Psalm 139 we hear this from the Psalmist:

"For you created my inmost being;

You knit me together in my mother's womb.

I praise you because I am fearfully and wonderfully made;

Your works are wonderful, I know that full well.

My frame was not hidden from you

When I was made in the secret place,

when I was woven together in the depths of the earth.

Your eyes saw my unformed body;

*All the days ordained for me were written in your book
before one of them came to be."* [5]

Stop for a minute and wonder at these words. God
created you as you are; you are fearfully and wonderfully
made. You don't need to compare yourself to others because
God has made you as you are - to be the person that you are
meant to be. And He knows you intimately as your creator.

I hope that, like me, this has led you to say the Wow
word! It does this to me every time I read these ancient
words. If we have to put up a pretence with others, we don't
with God; if we sometimes feel that we are just one of the
huge mass of humanity and don't really matter, we can know
that God knows and loves us as an individual. That is what
making our Home with God is all about; just as our home is a
place where we can be truly ourselves without pretence, that
unconditional acceptance and love is what we encounter
when God is our Home.

So, what difference does this make in reality? For me
this is a tremendous truth about honesty; that I can come
to God just as I am, without having to pretend at all. I can
come to Him and just let Him know what's going on; tell Him
how I am genuinely feeling without worrying I'm going to be
judged. And the process of doing that – or prayer, can help
us to come to terms with what is going on. It can help us
to know that despite everything else, He cares and is with
us throughout it all. This truth enables me to know a peace
that is beyond my understanding; when all around me is not
peaceful, I can know God's presence and His peace.

So, I Am at Home with God in the knowledge that He
knows me as a truly special individual. My dear old Dad, if I

---

5   Psalm 139:13-16 NIV

phoned him up and said: "Hi Dad it's only me", would reply with these words: "It's never only you – you are very special". He was right, because to God we are all special we are all truly known; we can be ourselves, because He knows us intimately. And we can then live out our lives with Him as He intended us to, but we'll discuss that a bit later on in the book.

Questions for reflection:

What times have you had a sense of wonder or otherness?

How do you respond to St Augustine's words – is there any resonance in your life of wondering if there is more?

Home is a place of peace and love
Nikki, Buckinghamshire

Chapter 3

Home is being loved unconditionally

Key to being truly known is love. But how do you define love? It's a very difficult task as there are so many meanings that describe the simple word 'love'. We love to do something, or we love our favourite food, wine, holiday destination, TV programme. The list could be endless. But possibly when we think of being at home, and of love, we think of the meaning of love as it embodies the care, compassion and intimate relationship between husband and wife, partners, parents, children and wider family.

When I was a curate, I ran a mock wedding with Year 1 children (aged 6) from the local school in the village church. There was a great degree of fun in this from the clothes chosen to be worn and bunches of flowers to be held, but what caused the most controversy was deciding who was going to marry possibly the prettiest girl in the class. At the end of the proceedings though, having heard an explanation of it all, I heard one little boy say to another "Nathan has just promised to look after Danielle for the rest of her life - that's wicked isn't it?" I was so pleased that the boys had really grasped the amazing pledges that are contained within the wedding service; promises to share and practise love no matter what happens to them, for better for worse, for richer for poorer, in sickness and in health.

Of course, the married relationship and expressions of love within the married vows are only one way that love is expressed at home. We can have intense relationships with all those we end up living with at home, whether we are married or not. Though, perhaps the relationship that speaks most of unconditional love is the parent child relationship. Parenting is based around that love. I don't parent my child to get something out of the relationship but I parent because I love – in an ideal world, simply that. If I insisted in order to win my love my child had to do something, this would become a conditional relationship not an unconditional one. So, perhaps it is this relationship that we can reflect on how being At Home with God is a place of unconditional love.

There is a meme on social media which says something like this: "If you want to know what unconditional love is get a dog!" Dogs often give devoted love to their humans and can show loyalty when others seem not to be loyal. But when I analyse my relationships with my dogs, I do wonder how much of that love is associated with the fact that I go to the cupboard twice a day to feed them, and regularly, in all weathers, put on my wellies and get their leads out to take them for some exercise. Just like a relationship with a dog, it is difficult sometimes to disentangle unconditional love from something which gives us many benefits. I joke with my family sometimes when I want them to make me something like a cup of tea, saying: "If you loved me you'd do that". To which the reply often comes back: "If you loved me you wouldn't ask". So, despite our best intentions even our unconditional love can be infused with self-interest.

For most of us, home and our family relationships give us opportunities to offer and receive unconditional love, although I want to acknowledge that some will have memories that are negative or even abusive. As I said in the introduction, for the most part, I had a very happy childhood with parents who gave of themselves in very many different ways and who I knew would love me unconditionally. There were times when I am not sure they liked me very much, or my behaviour, but I know that they never stopped loving me despite these things. But I know, for many people, family life won't have started that way, and sadly many grow up in homes where the love that parents have for their children is not enough to ensure their safety or happiness. We know that many people do not have the resources mentally or physically to care for their children in an appropriate way. The sad reality is, therefore, that some children grow up not safe physically or emotionally and to their true potential.

Whilst it is important to acknowledge that within every human home there is frailty and that trauma can occur for a variety of reasons, it seems to me that the concept of home is one where ideally the majority of people would experience unconditional love. It is with that model in mind that this analogy of home fits in with my faith in a God who loves me without reservation, totally unconditionally. No matter what I do, say, think, or how I behave He will never stop loving me. Furthermore, even if your human and earthly experiences of love have been disappointing or harmful, God's offer of unconditional love is freely and generously available to all. Here are some ways in which this love is described in the Bible; verses which I find helpful to read slowly and ponder.

Know therefore that the Lord your God is God; he is the faithful God, keeping his covenant of love to a thousand generations of those who love him and keep his commandments.[6]

Though the mountains be shaken and the hills be removed, yet my unfailing love for you will not be shaken nor my

---

[6]   Deuteronomy 7:9 NIV

covenant of peace be removed," says the Lord, who has compassion on you.[7]

But you, Lord, are a compassionate and gracious God, slow to anger, abounding in love and faithfulness.[8]

The LORD appeared to us in the past, saying: "I have loved you with an everlasting love; I have drawn you with unfailing kindness.[9]

And so we know and rely on the love God has for us. God is love. Whoever lives in love lives in God, and God in them.[10]

During Jesus' three years of ministry on Earth, He often told stories to the crowds that gathered, hoping to hear words of wisdom from Him. He used these parables to illustrate the nature of God's love and the way we too might live our lives practising unconditional love.

Parable of the Lost sheep:

Jesus told this story about a shepherd who, finding only 99 of his 100-strong flock of sheep safe, searched high and low to find the missing sheep. When he got back carrying the escapee safely to his fold, he then called his friends to celebrate. That's the very brief version. I love telling this story to children and taking bags of time showing how the shepherd searched high and low, calling "here sheepy sheepy", until he heard a little bleat in the bushes. But I have to say, when I imagine this story, I always also imagine nice clean fluffy white sheep; the sort you might find at the county agricultural fair. But actually, out in sheep farming country, one finds a rather scruffier sort of sheep, often covered in dirt and detritus, with half its fleece hanging off and in need

---

[7]   Isaiah 54:10 NIV
[8]   Psalm 86:15 NIV
[9]   Jeremiah 31:3 NIV
[10] 1 John 4:16 NIV

of a good shearing. If you read the story of the shepherd searching for this sort of a sheep, the story can take on a different sort of meaning. It isn't about the fact that it's the prize sheep that's been lost, the best bred, or the one with the whitest coat, but it's about any and every sheep that's been lost – probably a very mucky sheep with a habit of wandering off and getting itself into trouble. Jesus tells this story as He says to show that His Father rejoices in one sinner that repents because He loves them all.

So, the Parable of the Lost Sheep illustrates something amazingly profound about God's love; it is completely unconditional and is readily available for all. There is an engaging way of encountering Bible stories with children called Godly play. In this method you tell the story using small figures laid out on a mat on the floor. At the end of the re-telling of the story, the children are asked to think about questions beginning with "I wonder..." to help them reflect on the story. One such question which I remember striking me as an adult was this: "I wonder how the sheep who had been found felt when he was back safe with the flock?" How would you answer?

The Prodigal Son

This is another of Jesus' parables which many are familiar with, and which many artists have illustrated in rather wonderful ways. The story is interesting because it concerns two sons, and yet we pay attention to the son who goes away. The reaction of the supposedly good son, who stays home helping his Father, is interesting too and also speaks to us of God's love in a very profound way.

So, another brief version of the parable. The wealthy Father is approached by one of his sons who wants his inheritance now rather than waiting for it. The Father, disappointed, gives it to him and the son whizzes off to have fun with it. We hear he squanders it all and ends up looking after pigs, becoming so hungry that he has to eat their food; the ultimate shameful existence for a Jewish boy. So, he decides to go back home and ask for a job because he realises his Father would treat him better as a servant than others might. But on his return, the Father is elated to see him coming and welcomes him back as his son, calling for a feast to celebrate his return. The other son, though, isn't at all happy about this, but the Father discounts his hurt and sense of injustice, simply declaring his love for both his sons.

Here, the love and acceptance of the Father is totally unconditional. As a parent, if this happened to me, I think I might want to put some conditions on the return of my prodigal; perhaps expecting them in some way to pay back what they have lost. But here we just see the Father's love and acceptance of both the sons. Despite everything he has done, the son is back with his Father. He is accepted, he is loved, he is forgiven, and he is reinstated into the relationship with his family. Jesus tells this parable to further illustrate the total unconditional love and forgiveness of our Father God.

So, what about the "good" son? Was he right to feel aggrieved with the reaction of the Father to his brother? The unconditional love of God goes against the grain for most of us in many ways. I am sure we can find sympathy with the "good" son; after all he seems to have been there all the time and not squandered anything. We find it hard to accept this in terms of fairness because we judge so much of life by what we think is deserving. And yet, God's love is beyond our human comprehension, and challenges our thinking in so many ways. With God's love there is no sense of deserving because none of us can earn it or deserve it in any way, but it is just given to us freely – totally unconditionally.

Jesus' death and resurrection

This total unconditional love leads us to a hill just outside Jerusalem and three crosses, and in the middle was Jesus. You see, God's total unconditional love was shown by Jesus in how He dealt with others in His earthly life. This love was talked about by Jesus and demonstrated in His teaching and His parables, but ultimately this unconditional love was expressed fully by Jesus when He died on the cross for us.

In John's gospel we hear Jesus say these words:

My command is this: love each other as I have loved you. Greater love has no one than this; to lay down one's life for one's friends. You are my friends if you do what I command. I no longer call you servants, because a servant does not know his master's business. Instead I have called you friends. [11]

Perhaps you are familiar with these words from services on Remembrance Sunday where we think of those who have laid down their life for their country. And yet these words spoken by Jesus foreshadow what he was about to do. If the creation account shows us that we have separated ourselves from God, the crucifixion shows the way that God has put it all right, or redeemed us. As Jesus, totally without sin, died on the cross, He took with Him all the things that we have ever done and will do, and reconciled us to God.

When Jesus died on the cross, He died for each and every one of us. We all have in different ways fallen short of God's plan for our lives, and His death puts all this right. The horrific events of the crucifixion as told in the gospels bring me to my knees each Good Friday when we remember them once more. Yet small details offer us hope, even before the resurrection of Easter Sunday; for example, the tearing of the temple curtain. Before the crucifixion, God was thought

---

[11] John 15:12-15 NIV

to dwell only in the Holy of Holies within the temple, an inner sanctum only the priest was allowed to visit on special occasions to meet with God and to offer sacrifices. At the crucifixion when Jesus died we are told that the temple curtain, which separated God from the people, was torn in two; not as we would expect from the bottom to the top, but from the top to the bottom. A vivid demonstration that God is no longer separate and just to be found in the temple's Holy of Holies, but of a new direct-access to God, freely available to all. Because of Jesus' death we can know His presence as we are reconciled to Him, and we can invite God to make His home with us.

But the crucifixion of Jesus isn't the end of the story. Let's read some more famous words here, again from John:

For God so loved the world that he gave his one and only Son, that whoever believes in him shall not perish but have eternal life. For God did not send his Son into the world to condemn the world, but to save the world through him.[12]

The accounts of the first Easter Sunday when we see the appearances of the resurrected Jesus, show again His unconditional love. His triumph over death, and the resurrection of life itself, seems to be the absolute expression of God calling us to be 'At Home with God'. This unconditional love expressed through the death, life and resurrection of Jesus enables us to know the assurance of eternity with God Himself now. Fully At Home with God now and for eternity.

Questions for reflection:

How would you describe the Bible verses on God's love? Could you write a sentence that might sum up God's love for yourself?

---

[12] John 3:16-17 NIV

How might these parables speak to you – what do you wonder about them?

Home is a place of wellbeing

Phil, Hampshire

Chapter 4

Home is where I learn to forgive, and be forgiven

Being loved unconditionally is hard to take sometimes. Many of us often don't feel very loveable as we get things wrong so many times. However, alongside this unconditional love comes the ability to be forgiven, and to learn to forgive for ourselves.

On a recent walk by a lake, I saw a little girl sat quietly on a rock with her Mum looking on from a short distance away. The little girl was sort of whimpering and she seemed somewhat upset. Chatting to the Mum, I found out that she was having time out. Apparently, for the weekend they had been staying near the lake, she used this rock as her "thoughtful space".

I really like the concept of a thoughtful space, rather than a naughty step as is so often seen in TV documentaries about parenting. A thoughtful space seems a much more positive way of approaching how we get things wrong in life. A thoughtful space speaks to me of time to reflect and to think about our actions, and to come to a point where we might want to respond in a different way. The naughty step, in contrast, seems that it could be seen as a punishment. I guess they are the same thing, but the language we use does influence our perceptions. I am not sure I would want a naughty step in my home to use, but I wonder if we all need thoughtful spaces in our own homes.

Reflecting on our actions is just one of the ways of learning that we can use in our homes. Children learn and develop mainly through their homes and their interactions with their families. At home, we learn what is acceptable behaviour and what is not. We learn how to communicate with others, how to show thankfulness, how to demonstrate love and be loved. And I think one of the great learnings we have with our children is that of saying sorry and knowing that you are forgiven for the times you get things wrong.

As a parent and as a health visitor, I was a great advocate of setting clear boundaries for behaviour. Boundaries are important for us to learn because we generally push right up against them and yet these boundaries can keep us in a safe place. But often, even when setting boundaries, our children can overstep them in some way. Watching families interact, it is clear how often boundaries are pushed and pushed. The interaction of siblings can be fun too, as one winds up the other to overstep the boundary and then gets into trouble with the parent or carer. Then the fun starts as the phrase "Mummy, she just did that" comes into play, and the poor parent must react in a way that is fair to both children. Perhaps the Mum will call in the thoughtful space to get both of them to reflect on their behaviour. Or, perhaps like my own mother did to my cry of "Mummy he just hit me", she might reply, " I'm not surprised, I feel like doing that sometimes too."

My poor Mum, with four of us under 6 years of age, had a hard time of it when we were growing up, and I don't blame her for this response to me. But it does reflect to us that no matter what age we are, we don't always get things right, and we can get just as wound up by others as when we were children. I can reflect on others and see their faults easily, but often in life I need to have a thoughtful space to reflect on my own behaviour and actions. Perhaps the way I have reacted has been unhelpful to someone else, perhaps my words or actions have offended. In very many and different ways I can cause hurt and react wrongly.

As we reflect on our actions, at times we need to ask for forgiveness. This is something we have to learn to offer to others, but forgiveness is also something we need to accept for ourselves. Forgiveness is powerful in that it can put an end to bitterness and resentment. We see this demonstrated, very occasionally, when someone has had a great tragedy caused by another individual and they are able to offer forgiveness to that person.

But in the Bible, we hear of how we all need forgiveness, not just from each other but from God himself. In the Bible, God's standards are set out in the Ten Commandments. But Jesus, in His teaching on the sermon on the mount, brings these to life by showing how they relate to our attitudes and thoughts. When we judge ourselves against the Commandments, then we are all left wanting. We may not physically commit murder, but there are times when we think of someone else in a very negative light. We may not commit adultery, but there might be a time when we see someone and have a lustful thought. I could go on and on – but I hope you get the picture. However much we fail to live up to God's standards, the amazing thing about God is that through His unconditional love He will forgive us all the things that we have done wrong. He says these words in Isaiah:

Come now, let us settle the matter,"
says the Lord.

"Though your sins are like scarlet,
they shall be as white as snow;[13]

---

[13] Isaiah 1:18 NIV

When I was a teenager, I used to occasionally take the train into London for the day with a friend. If we were around Oxford Street, we would often see an older man walking up and down with a sandwich board which said these words "Repent for the Kingdom of Heaven is near." We used to be somewhat amused at this man, who obviously felt he had a real mission to tell the masses of Londoners and visitors the errors of their ways. But somehow this approach didn't really cut it for me.

This approach still doesn't cut it for me, as I think the approach of Jesus was so different from this. When I look at Jesus, I see Him getting to know them first before challenging them about their behaviours and the things they do wrong. In Luke's gospel[14] we have an account of Jesus going out with fishermen who were later to become his disciples. Before Jesus went out with them, they had been fishing all night and hadn't caught a thing. Jesus, though, tells them to throw the nets on the other side of the boat. After what is then a miraculously colossal catch of fish, Simon, recognising that Jesus must be something special, says to Jesus that he is not worthy to be in his presence because of his sin. Jesus then reassures Simon and sets him on a new way of thinking and being, as a disciple of Jesus, catching men not fish.

For some reason, we have in the Christian religion heaped blame and guilt on individuals before allowing them to encounter love and forgiveness for themselves. In the Middle Ages, we saw extreme examples of people trying to stop themselves from sinning by wearing hair shirts or even whipping themselves. This guilt is a mixture of how we perceive ourselves and how we think others perceive us. Perhaps it is also to do with the fact that we are very good at pre-judging others who are different from us; the basis for

---

[14] Luke 5:1-11

what we would now know as prejudice. I don't see this aspect of blame and guilt in the life of Jesus though. He befriends first, and then the encounter itself shows others where they are going wrong.

There are few people I have met in my life who I have really considered as holy. I have in my mind a dear friend who died a few years ago, and who was only in my life for a few years when I moved into my parish in Poole. He had been a fisherman and continued to take his boat out to catch lobsters into his 80s. But he was a very holy man. You knew when you met him that he welcomed you in a way that others didn't. He didn't judge you in any way and treated everyone as totally equal. He showed a care and compassion for others that was well beyond what most people would have expected, and all of this came out of his faith in Jesus Christ and his love of God. When you were with him you wanted to be different; you realised it wasn't going to be a good idea to have a conversation that was negative about another person, as he would not be interested. You saw in him how perhaps your welcome of others hadn't been as warm and genuine.

When we encounter true light, we see into the dark places of our lives. I think this is what happened when people met Jesus too. By the way He lived out His life, His conversation with others, His welcome to all, His care and compassion, others knew that they needed to change, and they were not living in a good way – the darkness was exposed by the light.

There is a lovely account of Jesus interacting with the tax collector Zacchaeus.[15] I love this story, as I learnt it as a child along with the simple way of telling the story in a little song.

Zacchaeus was a very little man, and a very little man was he,

---

[15] Luke 19:1-10

He climbed up into the sycamore tree, for the Saviour he wanted to see.

But when the Saviour walked that way, he looked into the tree

And said "Zacchaeus now you come down, for I'm coming to your house for tea."

The story starts with Zacchaeus climbing in a tree, presumably that means, he was too short to see over the top of the crowds. But Jesus stops and notices him and invites Himself to his home.

The song stops there, but the Bible story continues, and in it we see Zacchaeus responding to this visit from Jesus. We know that tax collectors weren't liked in first century Israel, not only because they were in collusion with the Romans, but because they would charge extra and keep a fair amount for themselves. So, the story continues with the people criticising Jesus for spending time at Zacchaeus' house. But we see Zacchaeus responding in a dramatic way to his encounter with Jesus:

But Zacchaeus stood up and said to the Lord, "Look, Lord! Here and now I give half of my possessions to the poor, and if I have cheated anybody out of anything, I will pay back four times the amount."[16]

Jesus showed Zacchaeus real acceptance by going to his home. In return, Zacchaeus' reaction shows that he has received forgiveness, and has decided to turn around his life in response to this. We are not told what was said by Jesus to Zacchaeus, but his action implies it all. He would only have done what he did if he had grasped the amazing acceptance by Jesus. Others wouldn't have anything to do with him, and yet Jesus accepts him and shows him forgiveness.

---

[16] Luke 19:8 NIV

I wonder if the story of Zacchaeus should act as a model for us all. I am not sure we would need to climb trees, but we could, like Zacchaeus, take a look to see what Jesus is about. The gospel accounts of Jesus show us the man Himself and His values, His compassion, His love and His forgiveness. And I wonder when we look at this, if we could know, like Zacchaeus, the amazing truth that God forgives us for everything we have ever done, and will ever do, and wipes our slates clean. All we need to do, like Zacchaeus, is accept that and respond in a new way to life itself.

Questions to Reflect:

Have you met anyone in your life who you would say reflects light? What was it about them that was so special?

How does the word forgiveness resonate with you and your own life? Are you in need of a thoughtful space in your life for reflection?

Home is a haven

Sandy, Dorset

Chapter 5

Home as a place of Safety

In peace I will lie down and sleep,
for you alone, Lord,
make me dwell in safety. Psalm 4:8[17]

What is a safe place? Personally, in my spiritual life, it is a place where I am known, loved and forgiven by God. In this way I can lie down in peace and sleep as we have just seen from Psalm 4.

Over the period of the pandemic, we got used to messages to stay at home for our own safety and for the protection of others. Our homes were seen increasingly as places to pull up our drawbridges and protect ourselves from harm. In the case of protecting from an invisible virus, this was very literally the physical case. Of course, the message was also that by protecting ourselves we have stopped others from being at risk by over-stretching the health and essential services.

Over the years, we have become much more risk aware and risk averse in our society. When I was entering my early teenage years, it was deemed safe for us to ride our bikes into the countryside, and spend days out riding around, with a small picnic to have at lunchtime, and (of course) the

---

[17] Psalm 4:8 NIV

ten pence piece to phone home in an emergency from the delightful red phone boxes. Nowadays, in our risk aware society, this would not be deemed a safe thing to do with the busyness of roads and other unmentionable threats.

On a day-to-day basis, we regularly assess our risk probably without being aware of it. Living by the sea, I enjoy spending time swimming and occasionally sailing with friends. However, I am also the chaplain to the local RNLI lifeboat crew, a group of people I am incredibly proud to be associated with. When I spend time in the water, I assess my safety carefully to ensure that I don't get myself into trouble. Now, of course it would be terrible to do so anyway, but I am also aware of the ribbing I would get from the lifeboat crew once the emergency had drawn to a close, if they had to rescue me. I know I could trust the crew to rescue me if I got into trouble, but I'd rather not chance it, thank you.

There are risks associated with everything we do, and throughout our lives we put things into place to ensure we are safe physically. We are also tremendously blessed by those who keep us safe in our emergency services whether full time or volunteers. However, I wonder if rather than our physical safety, our sense of safety in our homes is generally more psychological and concerns our sense of mental health and well-being?

Haven, Sanctuary, Safe harbour - all these are words which were given to me to describe home. They all seem to describe a place of retreat for safety, when outside the home seems uncertain, worrying and even harmful. Our homes should be places where we recover and give us rest. In this way they are places where we allow our energy to recover and to renew when things are tough and difficult outside.

If our homes are for us places of retreat and safety how does this fit with the move of people to have home as their place of work? I wonder if this might affect our place of safety, as the life of the outside begins to impinge on our sanctuary, after all our working lives are often the parts of our lives that that trouble us and give us stress? The blurring of these boundaries is something we will need to negotiate to ensure that home continues to be a place of energy recovery, rather than merely energy giving.

If our homes are places of safety, then the analogy of our own private fortresses is useful to consider. Littered around our countryside are fortresses and towers which have been used over the centuries for protection. Often these towers or fortresses are in a high place to allow good vision of those who come to try to overtake and allow a good opportunity to fire arrows or canons. Although now mostly in ruins, you can still see the sheer thickness of the walls. It's possible to imagine how safe you would have felt inside with the drawbridges up, when being attacked by a gang of marauders.

One of the descriptions of God in the bible that speaks of safety is this:

> *The name of the Lord is a fortified tower;*
> *the righteous run to it and are safe.*[18]

The idea of God as a place of safety and the analogy of Him as a fortified tower is one which speaks very clearly of being At Home with God. This is an analogy that is repeatedly used within the Bible, particularly in the writing of the Psalms. The people who first used these songs or prayers (the Psalms) would have known the realities of a tough life. They knew from first-hand experience the attack of enemy nations. For them, this analogy of God as a protective fortress, was very important in their day-to-day struggles with life and survival.

---

[18] Proverbs 18:10 NIV

Often in the Old Testament, the writers perceive that God helps the Israelites to a physical victory when they encounter foreign nations. However, more importantly, throughout these stories is a sense of God's presence bringing psychological well-being. In the story of Moses, we see this quite clearly. Moses was an uncertain leader having had quite a dodgy past including committing murder. However, God chose him to lead the people of Israel from slavery in Egypt to a new promised land. Unsurprisingly he thought he was unworthy to do this and was looking for someone else to help him, so he came to God to ask for this. Here is a snippet of Moses' encounter with God:

Moses said to the Lord, "You have been telling me, 'Lead these people,' but you have not let me know whom you will send with me. You have said, 'I know you by name and you have found favour with me.' [13] If you are pleased with me, teach me your ways so I may know you and continue to find favour with you. Remember that this nation is your people."

[14] The Lord replied, "My Presence will go with you, and I will give you rest."[19]

God promised the uncertain, hesitant Moses that He would be with him to do the role that Moses was called to do. If you read the book of Exodus, you can see that the experience of Moses and the Israelites wasn't easy. Their time leaving Egypt was fraught with problems and a Pharoah who refused to let them go. They journeyed through the wilderness for 40 years before finally coming to a place where they could settle. But Moses led the people because he knew the reality of God's presence with him. Moses was equipped to do this by God's presence and the promise too of restoration.

I wonder if this is what it means to be "At home with God" in safety? Our lives will be blurred by things that

---

[19] Exodus 33:12-14 NIV

come to us from outside, that uproot us, cause us stress and to constantly re-evaluate the things we take for granted. Though, within this, being "At home with God" can give us a sense of safety and security; that despite the things we face, that we know the presence of God is with us, to give us the ability to handle things, but also to give us restoration. If we are truly known and truly loved unconditionally by God, we can have a sense of security and safety within this.

This then leads us to consider the word 'peace' and the promise that God will give us peace if we trust in him. Peace is not merely an absence of trouble, noise or worry; peace is a deep-seated sense of well-being. If one Googles the word 'peace', you will be taken to a great multitude of quotes from many different world perspectives. The prevailing theme of these quotes, though, is the fact that peace is an inner state of being.

Amongst this multitude of quotes, you will see many from the Bible. The word peace is used in the King James Version of the Bible 429 times. Most of the times the word peace is used is to describe the feeling when we know and trust God. This can be seen here by Isaiah:

> *You will keep in perfect peace*
> *those whose minds are steadfast,*
> *because they trust in you*[20].

In the story of the calming of the storm, we see Jesus almost enacting this sense of peace in a physical way. He was tired and we are told that He went out with the disciples onto the lake and soon He was asleep in the stern of the boat. As the Sea of Galilee is surrounded by hills, and can act like a funnel for wind, not surprisingly a great storm blew up. Those

---

[20] Isaiah 26:3 NIV

manning the boat were experienced fishermen, but even they were scared. Eventually, they shouted to Jesus to wake up and do something. And to their surprise He commanded the storm to be still, using the words *"Peace be still".*[21] I often wonder if they hadn't woken Jesus up would they have still been safe? Jesus was with them, and He bought peace to the physical situation when they woke Him, but would just His presence in the boat been enough to keep them safe? Did the disciples show a lack of faith in waking Him up? Perhaps you might like to read this story for yourselves and ponder these questions, you can find the story in Mark 4:35-41

As Jesus came to the end of His earthly life, we see His care and concern for those close to Him. He knew the dangers that His followers would be in. To be a follower of Jesus was risky when He was alive, but also when He was gone, they would be seen as the ones causing insurrection. At the same time as this danger from the authorities, when Jesus left His disciples, they were going to have to deal with His loss, and at the same time try to do as He had taught them. Jesus knew all these dangers and troubles that they would face; He cared deeply for His disciples and His prayer before He is arrested shows this:

[14] I have given them your word and the world has hated them, for they are not of the world any more than I am of the world. [15] My prayer is not that you take them out of the world but that you protect them from the evil one. [16] They are not of the world, even as I am not of it. [22]

This is a prayer of protection for those closest to Him. It is a prayer that, like Moses, they would know God's presence. Before, they had literally been in the boat in a storm with Jesus and seen His power and His peace enacted, as He stilled

---

21 Mark 4:35-41 KJV
22 John 17:14-16 NIV

the storm with the word 'peace'. Now, as He gets ready to leave them, He prays that they would continue to know that presence in a spiritual way, as they stepped out to show the world the message of Jesus.

This chapter opens with the words of Psalm 4. Words which are said regularly within the simple service of Evening prayer. They speak of the peace which we can receive when we are safe "At Home with God". We can know this peace because we are loved unconditionally and known at the very core of our being. And if we trust Him, He is able to bring us peace despite the storms of life when we are truly "At Home with God."

Questions to consider:

How can we ensure our homes are energy giving rather than energy sucking when we blur the boundaries between work and home?

Reflect on the words at the beginning of the chapter from Psalm 4, what strikes you and can you relate to them in any way?

Home is where the people I love belong

Lizzie, Buckinghamshire

Chapter 6

Home is where the heart is

In our homes we experience key relationships. These relationships are often deep and intimate, and when these relationships work well we are safe both physically and emotionally. We move now to begin to see the invitation that God gives us to a sense of intimacy and belonging with Him.

The distinction between home as where we live and home as an emotional feeling is made clear in the phrase "home is where the heart is". Elvis Presley famously sang this song in 1962:

> *Home is where the heart is*
> *And my heart is anywhere you are*
> *Anywhere you are is home*[23]

The sentiment behind this song is, of course, the romantic relationship between two people. The notion that when you are in love, the other person will always be home to you. However, this phrase can be seen to refer not just to the romantic relationship but to the relationship with our families and those who are close to us.

The phrase 'home is where the heart is' probably originated in the early first century by Pliny the Elder and has been used in literature ever since. This small phrase

---

[23] Home Is Where the Heart Is lyrics © Gladys Music, Casa David Music

encapsulates the concept that home is not merely where we live – that is a house, or building, but home is a feeling. Home is where our affections lie, where we feel loved and love others in return.

As mentioned before, there can be a difference between where we live and where we are at home. We can refer to going home as returning to the place where we grew up or where those closest to us live. For some people, for a variety of reasons, home can be a place where they may not have ever physically lived but they have a particular affinity to it. So, the concept of home can be a place where memories of relationships reside – home is where the heart is.

I love the use of the word 'heart' in this phrase, as we all know that the sign of a heart indicates love. St Valentine's Day not only abounds with red roses but red hearts as couples indicate their love for each other. Within social media we use the heart emoji regularly to indicate that what has been posted online is very special to us. The shape of a heart we use almost reflects the shape of a human heart.

The heart is a vital organ in the human body. Without the pumping of our heart the other organs in the body will fail and life will not be sustainable. The heart is a muscle which ensures that the flow of blood round our body happens through the network of veins and arteries. If our heart begins to fail, the fluid in our body backs up and we are left with problems of circulation and congestion. If our heart stops, then very soon areas of our body will not get the levels of oxygen they need to survive and will die off. In short, even without extensive medical training, it is possible to see that the functioning heart is vital to our physical wellbeing.

But our psychological wellbeing is also deeply affected by the heart, which represents love. If the physical heart promotes good health, the amount of love we feel and give out also affects our mental health and wellbeing. We were made with the capacity to love, without love we do not develop to our full stature as humans. The Beatles might have been right when they sang "all we need is Love".

If home is where the heart is, then home is clearly seen as a place where love dwells. This is key also to our sense of living "At Home with God". When we know we are loved unconditionally, then we can rest in that love, and that becomes a place of "home". We can see this in the parable of the Prodigal Son and the sense of the Son coming home to his Father and being accepted back, not only into the family home, but into the love and acceptance of the Father.

In abstract sculpture, where the detail of the image is abstracted, the emotions that are portrayed can be exquisitely represented, present and poignant in the smooth stone or bronze by the artist. In the Washington National Cathedral Gardens there is a sculpture of the Prodigal Son in Belgium Granite, by the artist Heinz Warneke. In this representation, the embrace of the Father and Son appears almost as one figure[24]. The lack of detail between the two bodies serves to show the innate love that is present and that is being lavished on the Son by the Father. When I look at this sculpture, I am reminded of the awesome way God lavishes His Love upon us; the Son is held; the Son is almost one with the Father, and would be able to feel his beating heart in the embrace. The story Jesus told, and this portrayal in granite, speak of the way we can rest next to the heart of God.

---

[24] George Matheson (1882) Public domain

In the mid-20th Century, a favourite wedding hymn would be 'O love the will not let me go'. Of course, although used in weddings, it doesn't really refer to the love that is celebrated at marriage between two people, but it is about the love of God:

> O Love that will not let me go
> I rest my weary soul in Thee
> I give Thee back the life I owe
> That in Thine ocean depths its flow
> May richer, fuller be[25]

---

[25] George Matheson (1882) Public domain

The words are full of meaning and represent the image of the Father and Son in the Prodigal Son; the love which is so part of us that it is difficult to see where we end, and it begins. The way this love is portrayed in these words speak of a love that will never let us down or forsake us, but a love that holds us and is overflowing in how it gives and gives to us.

St John writes poetically of God in these words, which we find in his letter in the Bible:

God is love. Whoever lives in love lives in God, and God in them.[26]

The interaction of God and mankind is made perfect because of the love that is innately part of God himself. This is quite deeply theological, but suffice to say that God has no way of being except to love. God's very nature is love. He has no way to be or to interact with mankind, except through love. We find this so hard to understand as it goes against what we know and experience. We as humans (although made in God's image) have the capacity to make our own decisions and grapple with our own selfish needs. Made in the image of God, we are people of love, but we are also flawed people. We turn away from a way of life that encapsulates love to a way of life that often seeks pleasure or success at the expense of others.

If we were truly people of love, then every part of our lives would be governed by how our actions affected others within our world. We don't have to look very far to see examples of how this is not the case. Often our selfish actions and need for a good deal can impact the lives of others. What about the desire for cheap, clothing which we discard after a season? Made for a pittance by those across the world in

---

26 1 John 4:16 NIV

often terrible conditions, and then dumped in huge piles along the shorelines of the third world. One example of many where we do not consider our impact on the lives of others.

But when we fail so often to be people of love the amazing truth is God is love; his actions are those of love itself. And so, if we are truly "At Home with God" we are at Home in His love, enwrapped by His embrace, and perhaps feeling the beat of His heart. Which leads us to the question how can we be in this place, truly At Home with God?

Question to reflect:

Where is your heart?

Home is shoes off, cat on lap, hot tea, hugs, giggles, adventure planning (and endless piles of washing!)

Suzie, Dorset

Chapter 7

Make yourself at Home

At the entrance to Liverpool Cathedral, above the west door, is a Neon Sign by the Artist Tracey Enim, with the words "I felt you and I knew you loved me."[27] When I visited the Cathedral, I was bowled over by this amazingly simple yet incredibly profound art installation. These words resonate at a very deep level with my own experience of being "At home with God." Why? Because for me my faith is based around the concept that I am deeply loved and held by someone who I can't see. Yet, this is not purely theoretical as I can recognise in my own experience that I am known, held and loved by God. For me that is truly what it means to be "At Home with God".

But this is not a passive experience but does require a response from ourselves to fulfil the ultimate desire of God Himself. In the book of the prophet Ezekiel, we hear God say:

My dwelling place will be with them; I will be their God and they will be my people. [28]

This is showing God's desire to make Himself at home with His people. He is wanting to be with them, for them to let Him be with them and to guide them. And this desire of God, to want us to make Himself at home with us, is still

---

[27] Image can be found at: www.liverpoolcathedral.org.uk/home/about-us/art-in-the-cathedral.aspx

[28] Ezekiel 37:27 NIV

as incredibly true now as it was when He said these words through the prophet Ezekiel so many thousands of years ago. So, what might it mean for us to open our lives to God so He can make Himself at home with us?

I am sure most of us have had the experience of being invited by another to make yourselves at home when you visit them. Receiving an invitation like this can, though, be somewhat confusing. Do they actually want us to treat their home like we would our own or is it on their terms? Does this invitation mean I have permission to raid the fridge and check the cupboards for hidden chocolate? Can I take my shoes off and leave them in the middle of the sitting room? Can I curl up with my feet on the sofa under the rug that's so handily placed in a designer fashion across it's back? I normally have a good look around the house before I respond and follow the subtle clues as to how the homemaker themselves behaves and makes themselves at home. I would try to treat their home with respect and care.

In the same way, an invitation to God to make Himself at home with us leads to respect and care. We might not see God Himself, but we can know His presence and feel His love just as these words express: I felt you and I knew you loved me. But the onus is on us, not on God. He will never force His presence upon us, but wants us to turn to Him to know His presence. And there may be a pile of different things and reasons that stop us doing this. Often, we don't think that God would want to have anything to do with us because of who we perceive ourselves to be. We have the idea that we must be a certain kind of person, living out a certain type of life, and saying the right sort of things for God to think we are worth bothering about. Yet when we measure ourselves up against this sort of imagined person, we are left wanting in different ways. We might not think we are worth it, we might not think we live a good enough life or say the right things. But, and it's a big but here, the unconditional love of God shows us that it is nothing about what we do but all about God Himself. He loves us unconditionally, He forgives us for all the things we have done, and He wants us to know that we are loved and truly known by Him. His love is beyond our understanding, and He wants us to turn to Him no matter who we are.

Sometimes in talks with groups of all ages, I ask my audience who wants a sweet from the bag I have in my pocket. I can guarantee that it will be the children in the group who will put up their hands. I challenge this, noting that there will be some adults who are rather partial to a rhubarb and custard sweet themselves, to which I get some stifled giggles and know I have hit a nerve. But the reality is the adults are dubious of my offer because they think I want something in return, or I might be up to some sort of mischief. We get cynical as we get older, don't we? The phrase 'there is no such thing as a free meal' is one we trot out when we are offered anything from a sweet by a harmless vicar to a free piece of double glazing.

Jesus was once surrounded by children and His disciples told them to go away and to stop bothering Jesus. In return Jesus told the disciples off and said:

"Let the little children come to me, and do not hinder them, for the kingdom of God belongs to such as these."[29]

I have always understood this as Jesus saying that children have a way of accepting things that adults have become very cynical about. Jesus offers a relationship with God that is free, and it doesn't warrant us doing anything. He calls us to accept this as a free gift. If we want to have a technical theological term for this we use the word 'grace'.

---

[29] Mark 10:14 NIV

God's love and presence is given to us not because we deserve it but because God wants to give it to us, and all we need to do is accept it. All we need to do is allow God to make Himself at home with us.

But then again what about inviting people into your home? I can try to make my home as comfortable as I can for others who may partake of my hospitality, but there are areas of my home that I would like to keep hidden. How many of us put away bits or pieces when we are entertaining so as not to give away too much of our lives? I remember clearly trying to sell our little flat many years ago in the middle of a property crash, and using various tricks to promote it such as the smell of baking bread. One evening I came back from work and not expecting any prospective buyers started to cook kedgeree, with a strong smell of both curry and fish; this was not on my list of tricks. To my consternation the estate agent buzzed the door and I had a moment to respond before he was walking up the stairs with an interested buyer. In an instance the kedgeree was hidden; it wasn't until after the visit that my husband asked me where I put it. I replied by opening a cupboard door in the kitchen area and saying that I had been praying the agent or potential buyer was not going to do the same. This is an extreme example but there are things and areas in my life that I don't normally want my visitors to see; parts of my home that are more personal, say my bedroom or even the upstairs bathroom where all my pots and potions might be contained.

If God truly knows us then He knows what we keep in those places in our lives that we might be a bit embarrassed about, just like those potions we keep away from others in our bathroom. If God truly knows us and loves us unconditionally then He accepts those things in our lives, even if they are not necessarily what we would want Him to see or know about.

He loves us and He wants us to know the reality of that love for ourselves. And we don't need to do anything amazingly special, just stop and ask Him to come and make Himself at home in our lives. He's done the hard bit already with the life, death and resurrection of Jesus that makes this all possible.

I learnt the reality of this when I was quite young having been brought up by parents who took faith seriously. But there have been times when I have been quite keen not to live "At Home with God". Other things have seemed for a time somewhat more interesting, more cool, easier to stay in the crowd with others. But knowing the love of God and the relationship that I have with Him has been the mainstay throughout my life, I have kept coming back time and time again. It's not been a static relationship there are times when I have felt I have moved forwards hugely in terms of my faith and living out my life as a Christian, but there are other times when I wonder what it's all about and whether I can honestly call myself by this name.

In the previous chapter, we thought about the story of Zacchaeus and Jesus' call to him to come to his house. What if Zacchaeus had said no? I wonder what would he have missed out on and how would he have kept feeling about the life he was living? The book of Revelation in the Bible is the vision of St John of the end times. It's a bit difficult to understand at times but there is a point in the vision where he sees Jesus knocking at a door and saying these words:

I stand at the door and knock, if anyone hears my voice and opens the door, I will come in and eat with that person, and they with me. [30]

The Pre-Raphaelite painter William Holman Hunt famously painted this verse with a very western Jesus at a

---

[30] Revelation 3:20 NIV

door with a lamp – the picture entitled Light of the world. However, when you look at the door you see that there is no handle on the outside of the door. Why? Because Jesus is waiting for the person inside to open it so there is no need for Him to be able to open it up Himself – He's not going to force Himself in He's going to wait for it to be opened.

So, the invitation is to all of us. Are we willing to open the door on hearing His voice and allow Him to make Himself at home in our lives? If so, we could truly be "At Home with God".

Questions for reflection

How does the idea that God might be able to know the whole of your life feel- even the bits you'd rather hide?

Have a look if you can at the painting by Holman Hunt – what strikes you about this picture?

Home is somewhere where you belong

Charlie, Durham

Chapter 8

Home is a place of belonging

When we allow God to make Himself at home with us then we begin another journey of discovery about who He is, and how our relationship with Him might change us in surprising ways. The rest of this book moves to explore this in different ways. It is not exhaustive, but begins a time of reflecting on how this relationship might grow and develop. But we start this reflection thinking about belonging.

Psychologists from Freud onwards have identified belonging as a key psychological need, and seen it as vital, not only in child development, but in the emotional well-being of any age. The psychologist Melanie Klein developed the hypothesis that by looking at the significant relationships in a in a person's childhood, it is possible to uncover how these early life experiences can contribute to understanding current relationships. The psychologist John Bowlby recognised the importance of attachment with another from infancy. Bowlby's theory developed the idea that attachment to another in infancy would be the foundation for forming other relationships. Alongside these theories is the work of Donald Winnicott who famously spoke of the "good enough" mother. All these theories point us to the importance of the relationships that we develop with others from a very early age. These relationships are pivotal in the ways that we develop psychologically and they help us form our identity.

But also, these theories point towards a secure base being a foundational point for child development.

From these psychological theories three words can be identified which help us to look at a sense of belonging that we might receive from our homes: inclusion, identity, and acceptance. By looking at these three areas of our lives we can draw from them how being "At home with God" can meet these needs in each of us.

Inclusion:

At school I hated PE particularly when there were team sports. Why? Because I was more artistic than sporty, and as a plump teenager was not the first choice to have in your team. Imagine the sight by the edge of the sports field with the PE Queens chosen to pick their teams, and me left on the side lines until the very end of the choices are made. It was unbearable, and very demeaning. Now, I was good at some things, but I felt a complete outsider when it came to PE and team games, and although included in the playing of them, much the time very reluctantly by the team captains, I never felt I was truly included.

At home though I felt a real part of a family. It wasn't always an easy place to be as the youngest of four siblings, but I knew that when push came to shove, my parents and siblings had my back and would continue to love and protect me. The inclusion at home meant I was party to the in jokes, the mock conspiracy theories, the love of banana custard, but also the deeper conversations that were had about faith, ethical issues and how we were to live out our lives.

The story of Jesus in the Bible begins with a sense of inclusion of all. The Nativity story contains some very interesting characters. The shepherds were the dregs of the society of the day; the wise men unknown men from a far-off land, not normally present in Bethlehem; and the innkeeper, a good Jew who just made some space, even though it was a stable. These characters vary so much and yet they are all included in the story. Why? Because in this we are being shown that Jesus was coming to bring something different and new, He was coming to open God's Kingdom so that all could be included no matter what race, gender, or place in society they came from.

The unconditional love of God means that we are accepted and included as part of God's own family. We are now called sons and daughters of God as St John writes:

See what great love the Father has lavished on us, that we should be called children of God! And that is what we are![31]

We belong to God and to each other. I like to think of the cross as representing this in a pictorial way. So, the vertical bar represents the relationship between me and God, and the horizontal bar, like two arms outstretched, representing the relationship between all those who know that they too are children of God.

Identity

Have you noticed on holiday how easy it is to identify those who are on specific tours? The hats, the headphones, the following of the big yellow umbrella indicates the identity of the tourists. There is a sense that they follow a prescribed pattern of being and of dress.

We form our identities from our experience of home life, but also from how we interact outside the home, and the friends that we relate too. Our life at home though is pivotal in giving us a sense of who we are and the values we hold. We might express our identity in different ways to our parents in

---

[31] 1 John 3:1-2 NIV

such things as dress, tattoos, piercings, and in our behaviour. If belonging to a family can give us a specific identity, then children that have been through the care system can struggle with this.

My identity within my family was shaken when I was a young teenager. My parents "last will and testament" had been made before I was born, and I found out that I was not listed in name but merely as "any other child" that my parents might have. The moment I found this out is etched on my memory as it felt so painful. I was on a family picnic and had to take myself off for a long tearful walk to calm myself down, recover from an enormous strop, and then work out my position within the family again. Of course, I now know that this had absolutely no bearing on my place within my family. But, at that time of this discovery, I could not see this, and so it deeply upset me. It was also not helped by the continued teasing of my siblings long after this incident.

Being "At Home with God" means that we now belong to God's family. This in turn gives us a new identity as His children. This is expressed beautifully in the Church of England Baptism Service where these words are said:

As children of God, we have a new dignity and God calls us to fullness of life.[32]

In my identity as a child within my family I display the values that have been developed from my life within this family and the interaction of others within it. In my identity as a child of God I need to display the values that I hold as part of God's family. Jesus said these words which are key to our understanding of how we are to live out our identity as God's children:

---

[32] Church of England Liturgy for Baptism Common Worship

[34] *"A new command I give you: Love one another. As I have loved you, so you must love one another.* [35] *By this everyone will know that you are my disciples, if you love one another."*[33]

The call to love is fundamental to a calling to be God's children and to live "At Home with God". Living out this calling, though, is hard, as we often come upon those who are difficult to love, even when they seem outwardly the same as we are. This is an outward sharing of the relationship that we have as children of God, a sense of working out our identity within God's family and beyond. Loving others may call us to be sacrificial at times, but following the steps of Jesus, it calls us to think of others and to replicate Jesus' compassion, care and mercy.

Acceptance:

"I shouldn't be here" you say in your mind when you arrive. Those in the room seem much more educated than me, or much more well-dressed than I am. They all seem to know much more about the subject we are here to discuss, or they are better friends with the person whose birthday we are celebrating, and I don't really know anyone else.

I wonder if, like me, this has been your experience at different times of your life. I often seem to struggle with this "imposter syndrome", of being in the wrong place or with the wrong group of people. Most of the time this is just my psychological perception of my own place and feeling, that I am not truly accepted or included as part of an elite club or group.

Belonging seems to be all about acceptance as well as inclusion and identity. We experience acceptance when we feel that we are valued and affirmed by others. It will only take one person to come and speak to me, and to have a

---

[33] John 13:34-35 NIV

conversation in which they seem genuinely interested, for my sense of imposter syndrome to die down.

At home, we are accepted for who we are as we experience the love of others who know us inside out. They might not always like what we do, but home is an environment when we work out those sorts of things, and compromise on idiosyncrasies and annoyances.

As we have said before God's unconditional love accepts us just as we are and he calls us his children. The apostle Paul writing to the Galatian Church expanded on this and spoke of us as adopted children:

⁴ But when the set time had fully come, God sent his Son, born of a woman, born under the law, ⁵ to redeem those under the law, that we might receive adoption to sonship.] ⁶ Because you are his sons, God sent the Spirit of his Son into our hearts, the Spirit who calls out, "Abba, Father." ⁷ So you are no longer a slave, but God's child; and since you are his child, God has made you also an heir.³⁴

The people who received this letter had a slightly different view to us of adoption. In Ancient Rome it was the practise of wealthy statesmen who had no heir to adopt a child who would then receive the estate at the end of the statesman's life. The child before had no entitlement to the estate, nor did he do anything to deserve it, but the good will of the statesman lavished this on him. Paul here speaks of how God accepts us just like this. He accepts us as His children and has given us all the benefits of such even though we haven't done anything to deserve this.

So now because of this acceptance we can know the presence of God with us. We can know God's infinite love and we can be part of the family of God. We are included, we are accepted and God has given us a new identity.

---

³⁴ Galatians 4:4-7 NIV

Questions for reflection:

Can you identify with moments when you do not feel you belong? How does this make you feel?

How does the Roman way of adoption and Paul's writing speak to you?

Home is a place to laugh, to be silly without feeling embarrassed and to share food, drink, thoughts, hopes and dreams with the family

Nicki, Dorset

Chapter 9

Home is a place of learning

Whilst home is a place of belonging, it also plays a major part in our development as individuals and in relationship with others. How much this nurturing contributes to us in contrast to our inherited nature is one of the oldest debates in psychology and theories of child development. This debate has always fascinated me when looking at my own children and in my previous role as a health visitor. The question is which factors, genetic or environmental, play a greater role in the influence of behaviour? Down the centuries both philosophers and psychologists have made arguments on either side. Although some theories may come down on a particular side, more common now is looking at the interaction of the two factors: genetic inheritance and environmental influence.

When I look at my own children I can see the influence of both genetics and environment. My two daughters have vastly different personalities in many ways. Yet, it is also possible to see characteristics of both myself and my husband in them both. As well as this, if you drill down you will see that they both hold very similar values and expectations of what they want out of life, yet they display these in their own individual ways.

So, you cannot fail to argue that nature has a distinct part to play in development, but nurture is very important too, and much of the nurture within development comes from the home. Before the pandemic of 2020, home schooling was very much on the sidelines. Because of the pandemic, parents suddenly had to get to grips with what it meant to home school their children. Stories abounded of the difficulties they found, and how to juggle demands of working life and home schooling. Some suggested ways of getting them learning whilst doing the housework, using cleaning fluids as a study in science, or cooking for home economics. Where children had previously seen school as their main place of learning, during the pandemic, home had to become the place.

And yet home has always been the prime place for learning in so many ways and in so many different aspects of life. One of the greatest things that is learnt in a home environment from a very early age is speech and communication. When a small baby makes a cooing noise, this is often echoed by the parent and in turn becomes the means of an early conversation. The meaning of words and the names of things are explained by picture books, nursery rhymes and trips out and about. By the age of two the vocabulary of children is well on the way to developing.

As well as speech, the clues for successful communication are also learnt at home. The use of non-verbal cues can be just as important to communicate well with others as speech itself, and these can be learnt from observation and from having to work out how to be involved in the conversation between parents and siblings.

So, home is undoubtedly a place of learning and development. When a home is not functional, and the child is not receiving adequate stimulation, the failure to develop at key stages can be a clear indication for professionals that intervention is needed. Home is a vital part in learning.

So how does home as a place of learning fit in with our theme of "At Home with God"? When we invite God to be at home with us, we need to find ways to develop different aspects of this in our lives. In any relationship we need to spend time with each other, learning from one another, and deepening that relationship, if the relationship is going to last for any time.

Deepening that relationship is all about deepening our roots. Walking recently through a Scottish wood I was surprised to see so many trees that had literally just fallen over within it. The wood had been planted so densely that the roots of the trees had not had enough room to spread out and develop into a secure root ball. When you saw the trees on the ground the lack of depth of the root ball was clear, it was shallow, and so the tree had not survived the storms and winds that had eventually led to its fall. To develop our living out "At Home with God" we need to take time to deepen that relationship and to ensure that our roots are secure in what we are doing, to cope with the stresses and strains of life. So, in this section I want us to consider various things which help us to develop that relationship.

Prayer

Think of a time when you have been together with others around a table perhaps having a meal or in discussion. As you remember the interaction remind yourself on how it developed; who took the lead, who was sitting on the sidelines quietly listening, and who was reacting to the conversation, and in what different ways? Any interaction can lead us to react in a variety of ways, and there are many ways to be part of a conversation. And yet when we think of prayer the danger is that we think of only one way of interacting: that of listing the things that we are concerned about. But prayer, like any communication is very multifaceted.

People often say to me when I am dressed in my dog collar: "say one for me will you". For some people I am, as a Vicar, the one who has prayer sewn up and I am therefore able to get to God quicker than most other people. But the reality is, that just like others, there are some times when prayer doesn't seem to come very easily. And to dispel all rumors, I certainly don't have a hotline to the Almighty.

But respecting the above, I can say that I have learnt over my own Christian life, to pray and to work out in a small way what prayer might be all about. There are loads of books out there which can help and have helped me over the years. Resources I cannot commend enough are the Prayer Course and the Prayer Course 2 available through the 24/7 prayer network, all great ways of discovering more about prayer. But for the purpose of this chapter, I want to start us thinking about prayer by looking at Jesus' own words:

5 "And when you pray, do not be like the hypocrites, for they love to pray standing in the synagogues and on the street corners to be seen by others. Truly I tell you, they have received their reward in full. 6 But when you pray, go into your room, close the door and pray to your Father, who is unseen. Then your Father, who sees what is done in secret, will reward you. 7 And when you pray, do not keep on babbling like pagans, for they think they will be heard because of their many words. 8 Do not be like them, for your Father knows what you need before you ask him.

9 "This, then, is how you should pray:

"'Our Father in heaven,
hallowed be your name,
10 your kingdom come,
your will be done,
on earth as it is in heaven.

¹¹ Give us today our daily bread.
¹² And forgive us our debts,
as we also have forgiven our debtors.
¹³ And lead us not into temptation,[a]
but deliver us from the evil one.[b] [35]

When I hear these words of Jesus in my mind I am taken into a courtyard, outside a synagogue, watching the goings on. You can just see the people he is talking about, can't you? The ones who are standing there (for some reason I imagine them very rotund) and praying very loudly and very earnestly in word, but they are all the time looking around to see if someone is watching them. And then you see others standing there going on and on in prayer and not really saying anything at all. But Jesus says we are not to be like these sorts of people, but that prayer is something that is between us and God and is something we do quietly, not making a big fuss.

When my Dad was alive I often used to speak to him on the phone, and we would catch up together for a good length of time. He was interested in what I was saying to him, and in our conversation, we would share news and he would offer advice on things I was going through. Generally, I had those conversations when I was on my own in a room of the house when others couldn't overhear. Why? Not because I was saying anything they didn't need to hear but because this was between Dad and me, no one else. I think this is just what Jesus is saying here about prayer to our Heavenly Father.

Then we have the words which most of us are familiar with in some way even if it was only from school a long time ago; the words of what we know as the Lord's prayer. This prayer is a great pattern for us to understand prayer

---

³⁵ Matthew 6: 5-13 NIV

and I want to break it down for us to see the depth of what prayer is:

Our Father in Heaven, hallowed be your name.

When I phone someone up, I don't normally start a conversation without a bit of an introduction. Here the words that Jesus starts with in prayer are an amazing introduction to remind ourselves of who it is that we are talking to. God, the creator of the world wants us to turn to Him to spend time with Him. God the creator of the universe wants us to get to know His will and plan for our lives. God our creator who made us for Himself loves us unconditionally. This is the God who we are now going to spend time with, our Heavenly Father who is Holy and worthy of praise and yet wants us to know Him personally. This introduction is important because it is reminding us of our place within the universe and the fact that we can turn to our creator God. We are sort of saying as we say "hallowed be your name", I'm in awe of you, I can only know a tiny bit of what you do and who you are but I am in awe that I can come to you and speak to you.

The words of Psalm 8 speak to this really powerfully:

When I consider your heavens,
the work of your fingers,
the moon and the stars,
which you have set in place,
what is mankind that you are mindful of them,
human beings that you care for them?[36]

[10] your kingdom come,
your will be done,
on earth as it is in heaven.

---

[36] Psalm 8: 3-4 NIV

I find it very difficult to be in a crowd of people and to listen to one conversation only as I get too distracted. I find it hard to block out other conversations that are going on around me, particularly if they seem more interesting than the one I am actually engaged in. I find it much easier to engage in a conversation when I am in a quiet place, with little else going on to distract me. Listening is an important part of a conversation, and God calls us in prayer to take time to be still and quiet too and to listen to what he might be saying to us. That is why this part of the prayer is so important.

By saying to God that we want the earth to somehow represent his kingdom in heaven, we are asking ourselves in these words what that might look like. What would it mean for God's Kingdom to be on earth? I think this is a question that God asks us to reflect on regularly as we live in a society which has an onus on making the most for ourselves and not for others, and where the strong always seem to find their way to the front, and the gap between the rich and the poor gets ever bigger. What would it be like for God's Kingdom to come?

Asking ourselves this question requires us to reflect and to align ourselves with God in some way and listen to how we might respond. In my town, the work being done for the homeless both by charities, churches and the statutory authorities was under threat by a Public Spaces Protection Order that was suggested by the Council. As I prayed about this, I felt that this was against the values of God's Kingdom where all are of equal value to God. Alongside this was the fact that yet again those most vulnerable in our society were being targeted as an annoyance. But I realised as I prayed that I had to work out how I could help answer my own prayer. Rather than merely praying about the problem I was struck that I could make a difference in a practical way too. I had a real sense of being called to do something about this as well as to tell God about it. God convicted me strongly that I needed to get positively involved in this, so I stuck my head out and wrote a letter to the council copying it into the local press news bureau. The resulting media interest was great and resulted in several radio interviews as well as a brief TV interview. Promoting this to the local churches and the media gave great kudos to the local homeless Charity and local interest and support was raised.

Often when we pray and stop, align ourselves with God's will, and listen, then we begin to see how we can be the start of an answer to that prayer. Even if our part is only small, God can use us to bring his Kingdom's values to earth as it is in heaven.

[11] Give us today our daily bread.

Who doesn't like a good loaf of bread? Bread is one of those bits of our diet that seems to be worldwide but expressed in different ways. From our farmhouse loaf to the flat breads of the Middle East, most of us in our homes will have bread of some sort or another; it is a staple in our kitchens.

Jesus tells us to ask for our daily bread each day. I think it's wonderful that He chooses something which is so worldwide in its appeal to be asked for rather than our daily yoghurt or other staples we might rely on in our diet. Jesus seems here to be saying to us ask for what you need today. Regularly come to God to ask for what you need.

Generally, this is the bit of prayer that we are reasonably good at. We formulate our list of what we want to ask God for, and we go through it for our own needs, the needs of others close to us and the needs of the world. This is where my hotline to God comes in handy particularly if it's to do with needing some sunshine for a special occasion! But I know there are at times when I pray in this way that I need to look at what is a need, and what is something that I want. Give us today our daily bread acknowledges that God provides us with what we need. Sometimes things happen that are not what we want but even in these situations, He gives us what we need to cope with this.

One of my favourite ways of praying for others is using these words as I speak the names of those who are suffering in some way or going through a pretty difficult time: May God meet them at their point of need. In other words, may God supply them this day whatever their daily bread is.

> [12] *And forgive us our debts,*
> *as we also have forgiven our debtors.*
> [13] *And lead us not into temptation,[a]*
> *but deliver us from the evil one.[b]'*

This last bit of the prayer that Jesus taught us seems to me about getting things straight with our lives. I think I'm quite good at navigating and am always reluctant to use SatNav unless I absolutely don't know where I am going. Often, I look at the map before I leave and spend the journey trying to remember which way to go. Sometimes it works out, but there are other times when I realise I have absolutely no idea where I am or where I am supposed to go; I have got it wrong big time. I have a choice at this point, blindly try to work out my way or switch my phone to Google maps and let Google take the strain out of the situation.

Sometimes, and as you may have noticed I am not always good at this, we must admit we have gone wrong and turn around and ask for help. Often in our lives this is to do with our relationships with other people or how we have reacted to different situations. Coming to God quietly and asking for

His forgiveness not only means we are straight with Him, but can then urge us to take time to go to those with whom we have wronged to say we are sorry.

Throughout this prayer from the beginning, we have begun to realign ourselves with God and to seek to know his will. This last bit of the prayer is very much about this. It would be ludicrous if we knew we were on the wrong road, and carry on blindly without a real idea of where we are going. In the same way, carrying on doing the things which we know are wrong: where we give in to the temptation of the world, where we upset other people, and so on is ludicrous. Taking time to acknowledge this sets us back on track, puts us on the right road again and enables us to continue our journey of faith.

As we learn to live out our time "At Home with God" and begin to pray we deepen our roots and are able to withstand more storms. But a further way is learning to read Gods word.

God's word – The Bible

Often, I am asked what the best way to start reading the bible is, and my immediate response is always "not at the beginning"! Just like when we learn to read when we are younger, often at home helped by our parents, we need to learn at our own pace and in ways that help us to understand not to completely confuse us. We need to learn by listening to others who have gone before us helping them to explain to us.

So how do you start reading the Bible if not at the beginning? My advice would be to get some help with this and to get a daily reading guide to help you on the way. Reading a few verses each day with an explanation and application for the day can be a very helpful way of getting into a routine and learning more about the Bible. Just like when we learn to read, we start small and slow, so I would advocate learning to read the Bible and absorbing God's word.

The Bible is a complicated book which contains amazing different genres and is a mix of history, story and parable, teaching, and guidance. At the heart of the Bible though is God's love for humankind. It starts and ends with this as we see from the creation in Genesis, to a vision of the end of the world in Revelation. The relationship between God and his people is at the heart of the history and story and the desire for them to know God spans the full breadth of this book. It's a bit like a history book, a love story, and a guide for how to live your life, all wrapped up in one cover. If you want to read a chunk then start with the stories of Jesus contained within the four gospels. They're a great read and you can learn so much about God's priorities and his Kingdom values by reading these.

There are many books and courses to help you with this and this is not the place to describe too much more. But, it is fair to say that living "At Home with God" you will deepen your relationship with Him if you start to read and take in God's revealed word to us written by so many people down the centuries in the Bible. So, what's stopping you? And by the way, the Bible has been top of the best sellers list of books in the world for the longest time, so you are not alone in getting it off your shelf and dusting it off and starting to read.

Pause to reflect:

How might it be possible for you to deepen your roots in prayer and knowing God's word?

What might you need to do to put this in place?

Home is somewhere where you can be yourself without fear of being judged. Where the people and things that are most precious to you are.

Rob, Buckinghamshire

Chapter 10

At home we display our values, and priorities

Learning to communicate and to deepen our relationships is vital for our development. Alongside this, at home, we also learn something fundamental to our identity in the values and priorities that we hold and live out.

One of my guilty secrets is to spend time looking at properties for sale on the web or to watch TV property programmes. It's fun to dream by looking at someone else's lifestyle, to imagine yourself in their space and to think how you might change things. But one of the things I love is to look for clues as to what priorities the person who owns the house might have in their lives. Clues might include the fridge and kitchen cupboards displaying childrens' art, or perhaps the elegant designer furniture, or even the mound of recipe books on the kitchen shelf.

Our homes display a huge amount about us, our interests and the things we see as priorities, these priorities are often learnt from our time at home as a child. Often these are picked up by our experience as children and the values held by our own parents or carers. Going to the home of a friend, when growing up, we can experience a degree of culture shock, as we notice a huge difference in behaviour to what we might be used to. This behaviour is normal for them, and mostly neither way or behaviour is right or wrong – it's just different in different homes.

From our experience of home life we react in different ways to what we have been led by others to view as important. Often, we react negatively, thinking we will never fall into the same traps that we perceive our parents have fallen into, such as the dominance of work. However, sometimes we will try to emulate behaviour, priorities and values.

The values we hold will clearly lead us to identify the priorities that we will have in how we live out our lives on a day-to-day basis. How much time, attention, physical, and mental resources we expand in different ways will very much depend upon our priorities. But what will our values be if we live "At home with God"? To answer this question, we have to look at what the Bible might say about a new way of living when we are in relationship with God.

Before I do this, I want to reassure you, that, against popular myth, God isn't a kill joy. Following his priorities isn't about being very boring and not having any fun. I hope my reflection here can show that living out my relationship "At Home with God" and holding God's priorities can be full of life, to nourish us and give us a real sense of fulfilment.

So, our Biblical reflection starts with the Old Law in the Old Testament, which we probably know best for the 10 commandments.[37] Moses encounters God on a Mountain and comes down with tablets of stone containing these commandments as a way of living for the people of Israel. In a largely secular society our moral law still seems based upon these commandments.

When I teach children about the 10 commandments, I use pictures of road Stop signs to help illustrate them. So, we have a stop sign when we are about to encounter some sort of danger: the edge of a quay, a railway crossing, a T junction. We

---

[37] Exodus 20:2-17 NIV

stop here to ensure we are safe, and we don't hurt ourselves and others. In the same way the 10 commandments stop us hurting ourselves and others.

I find it very helpful to think of these commandments as being not just rules for us to live by but things to stop us from being hurt. It always amazes me how different people interpret rules. We saw this clearly in the pandemic with different interpretations of things like bubbles or social distancing. I have always tried very hard to keep rules, but I have to say sometimes this is more because I fear being told off than because I think it's a good idea. So, seeing God's commandments to Israel as things to stop us from getting hurt and hurting others is calling on our sense of altruism rather than reacting in some way to regulation.

But the call to a new way of living does not end in the Bible with the 10 commandments. In Matthew's gospel we have a wonderful account of Jesus sitting on the side of a hill with those who are following him and teaching them about living out their lives. He challenges so many things they thought they were doing right, and goes beyond just not doing things to look at attitudes and deeply hidden emotions:

You have heard that it was said to the people long ago, "you shall not murder and anyone who murders will be subject to judgement." But I tell you that anyone who is angry with a brother or sister will be subject to judgement.[38]

This teaching in the Sermon on the Mount also gives His people the calling to be salt and light in the world.[39] Today

---

[38] Matthew 5:21-22 NIV

[39] Matthew 5: [13] "You are the salt of the earth. But if the salt loses its saltiness, how can it be made salty again? It is no longer good for anything, except to be thrown out and trampled underfoot. [14] "You are the light of the world. A town built on a hill cannot be hidden. [15] Neither do people light a lamp and put it under a bowl. Instead they put it on its stand, and it gives light to everyone in the house. [16] In the same way, let your light shine before others, that they may see your good deeds and glorify your Father in heaven.

we worry about having too much salt in our diet and we see the connection with our health. Therefore, we are advised to avoid salt, and yet which savoury recipes have you found that don't add seasoning with salt and pepper at the end? But in the days of Jesus, salt was an important commodity and one which was essential in a variety of ways. It was used to preserve things and was a hugely important for moving away from a total dependence on seasonally available food. Salt was, as it is now, also used as a seasoning to change the taste of something and to bring out the flavour. So, the calling of Jesus to His followers to be salt is a profound calling. They are people who help to bring transformation to society and to bring out a new flavour to the communities in which they live.

Added to the calling to be salt is also the calling to be light. The concept of light in the darkness is one which I think most of us associate with Christianity in particular with the time around Christmas when there seems to be a proliferation of lights shining and candles bedeck our churches. A light in the darkness can keep us safe along a dark road with the perils of potholes to navigate. A light is also a guide to us and can help us to know the way to travel.

But Jesus said these words in John's gospel – "I am the light of the world"[40] and elsewhere he says to his disciples – "You are the light of the world"[41]. In this amazing statement, Jesus is claiming His place as God's Son who will show us the way to live out our lives. His turning this back to His disciples shows that He sees them continuing the message of His light throughout their lives. This is very important as Jesus knew at this stage that He wouldn't around with them in person on earth. In other words, if we follow Jesus then we are to live

---

[40] John 8:12
[41] Matthew 5:14

out our lives trying to emulate Him in showing the priorities and values that He declared by His life. That is a huge calling but one which allows us to be the people that God intended us to be.

If we look at the life of Jesus, we see a pattern for living that is so different from the culture of the world around us. We see Him showing care and concern for those on the edge of society. We notice His challenge to the status quo, of those who felt they had power and authority due to their position and used it wrongly. His values are those of compassion, justice, and peace. There is a myriad of stories about Jesus where He challenges our assumptions of normality, and how we have been told by society to act and think. I guess the challenge for us all is to look at what He said and did and try to emulate, and to hold these values for ourselves in how we live out our lives.

My experience of trying to live out my life in this way is one which gives me great meaning. My sense of self-worth is no longer based on what other people think about me, or whether I am doing something worthwhile with my work life. In living out my life in this way then my priorities change to be much more about other people and showing care and compassion.

This might not come naturally and may be easier said than done. The pressure of society around us would say our values might need to reflect other things. The pressure of society might require us to expand our resources on things that are self-seeking rather than giving to others. But when the push comes to shove, what is important to you in your life? During the first lockdown of the pandemic in 2020, many people spoke about this showing us what was important in life. Lockdown took away our constant desire to go out shopping, or to the latest restaurant. It took us back to want to spend time with those we love, it took us back to wanting to help our neighbours. It took us back to a place of care and compassion and was a positive time in this way for many people.

So, after this time in our lives what have we returned to? Does how you spend your time and resources reflect your values and priorities? One of the things I say often when I am preaching is that if we want to find out our priorities in life, we need only look at our bank statement! In my experience, following the values of salt and light enables me to truly be the person I was intended to be, using my gifts and abilities for others and for the flourishing of all. So, following this new way of living when we are "At home with God", rather than being restrictive, enables flourishing and can nourish not only us but other people too, as we are salt and light in an often tasteless and dark world.

Questions to reflect on:

What would your bank statement say about your priorities?

What bits of Jesus' teaching and life would you find most difficult to take on?

Home is my/our personal space. Home is where I can be me, say and wear what I want without judgement.

Carole, Dorset

Chapter 11

Home is where I am able to shout and scream

There are very few places in reality where we can relax enough to be truly ourselves in how we act and behave to express the deepest of emotions. In my personal experience my home has been one such place. As a Christian I have also found that living "At Home with God" is a place, not only where I have grown and developed, but is a safe place to be truly myself.

2016 had been a good year in my life. Things were going well generally in both my personal and work life. My family were happy, and I was proud of where my children seemed to be heading. I was enjoying life; I was enjoying my work and I had even spent a few days away in my favourite place in France.

But, on the 23rd of November everything changed with the results of a call back after a routine mammogram. Going along to the appointment I wasn't too worried, as I had asked to have a lump investigated the year before, and although it was still present, I had been told then it was not sinister. But when I got to the appointment the looks on the faces of the various nurses and radiographers faces said it all. A diagnosis of breast cancer was just waiting to be confirmed by biopsy, but the consultant radiographer was clear that this was what to expect and to plan around.

In my first Staff Nurse post at Guy's Hospital in 1987, I had worked on the then research unit for Breast Cancer. I had seen women come in for initial diagnosis, treatment and then part of the ward was for those who were losing their fight against the disease. It had been a tough time as a young nurse, but one which I value as it gave me an amazing compassion for others, and an ability to sit alongside those who have received devastating news as well as the dying and their families.

My experience at Guy's though was some 30 years before my diagnosis and part of my coming to terms with what I was facing was to realise that things had moved on. I was told this by everyone I came across, but it was a difficult truth to hold on to as you struggled with the unknown. I was left for 3 weeks to wait for the appointment that would plan the treatment and those 3 weeks felt very hard going. The timing of this was excruciating too, my diary was packed full of Christmas events including a Tree festival with a gala cheese and wine evening which I was hosting. I was needed to be the smiling face of the Church when inside I was falling apart. Any energy I did have was making sure that I was covering my workload so that I could escape as soon as I knew what was happening.

I did a lot of crying and screaming in those weeks in the quietness of my home whilst putting on a brave face with those in my Church who had no idea what was happening. I remember walking back one night from a Christmas carol event and feeling the loneliest I had ever been in my life. I probably also felt the most exhausted from having to hold it together, work the crowd, and at the same time deliver some sort of message around the joy of Christmas. I came home and howled. Home then for me was a place of extreme safety. Everyone I lived with knew what was happening and they, and others close to me, were the ones who were supporting me through this time. As I howled, I was held by those around me who rocked me in their arms and said it was going to be OK.

Eventually, I was able to know a treatment plan and then go off sick for a while and let my Church family know what was happening. There was a huge outpouring of love as I went through my surgery and the subsequent radiotherapy treatment. My house was full of flowers, not just at the start, but for the whole 4 months I spent off sick. I knew very clearly that I was being prayed for during this time, which is just as well as I could do little spiritually for myself apart from repeating the following familiar words of reassurance over and over again:

The steadfast love of the Lord never ceases, his mercies never come to an end. They are new every morning great is his faithfulness.[42]

These words resonated so clearly with me during this time. They pointed to the fact that God was showing His mercies new to me each day and that I could trust in that. And I did. And in doing so I knew that not only were my family holding and rocking me in my pain but He too held me and His presence with me gave me strength.

Home is a place where, when we experience extreme pain, we share it with those with us, but we can also let go and just shout and scream and rage about what is happening to us. In the Bible I love to read the Psalms. This is a collection of poetry and song which was used in Hebrew worship and is used in Christian worship as well today. Some of the psalms are wonderful comforting words such as the famous Psalm 23 "The Lord is my shepherd". Words of comfort that speak of Gods sustaining presence like those in Psalm 121.

---

[42] Lamentations 3:22-23

I lift up my eyes to the mountains—
where does my help come from?
² My help comes from the Lord,
the Maker of heaven and earth.[43]

But a lot of the psalms display a real mix of emotions. Some of the psalms are known as psalms of lament because they speak of the emotional difficulty that the people are going through either on their own or in their community. Of the total book of Psalms around one third of them are in this genre. The words used in these psalms speak clearly of the pain that they are going through. They show deep loneliness and despair:

Look and see, there is no one at my right hand;
no one is concerned for me.
I have no refuge;
no one cares for my life.[44]

They display the depth of how the individual feels attacked by others physically or psychologically

Deliver me from my enemies, O God;
be my fortress against those who are attacking me.
² Deliver me from evildoers
and save me from those who are after my blood.
³ See how they lie in wait for me!
Fierce men conspire against me
for no offense or sin of mine, Lord.
⁴ I have done no wrong, yet they are ready to attack me.
Arise to help me; look on my plight!

---

[43] Psalm 121:1-2 NIV
[44] Psalm 142:4 NIV

14 They return at evening,
snarling like dogs,
and prowl about the city.
15 They wander about for food
and howl if not satisfied.[45]

They show the depth of pain that is felt:

Have mercy on me, Lord, for I am faint;
heal me, Lord, for my bones are in agony.
3 My soul is in deep anguish.[46]

So, we see the emotional extremes of life contained within the psalm from words of love to words of despair. Those who study literature will know that most poetry has a particular structure. This is also true in the psalms of lament which follow a structural pattern. You can see this quite clearly from Psalm 13. Here we have the struggle of the individual who feels rejected by God because of what they are going through. There seems to be a desire to find a meaning to his situation, and to see where God is within it. But the ending of the psalm seems to switch to words which in a way jar with those preceding them. In verses 5-6 we see the switch to words of trust and faith.

How long, Lord? Will you forget me forever?
How long will you hide your face from me?
2 How long must I wrestle with my thoughts
and day after day have sorrow in my heart?
How long will my enemy triumph over me?
3 Look on me and answer, Lord my God.
Give light to my eyes, or I will sleep in death,

---

45 Psalm 59:1-4, 14-15 NIV
46 Psalm 6:2-3 NIV

*⁴ and my enemy will say, "I have overcome him,"
and my foes will rejoice when I fall.
⁵ But I trust in your unfailing love;
my heart rejoices in your salvation.
⁶ I will sing the Lord's praise,
for he has been good to me.*[47]

So why this pattern? Psalms of lament are wonderful examples of faith in a God who is beside us even when we can't recognise that fact. There are often words that rail at God, that rage, that show despair, grief, and pain. But they are words of faith, as they show that we can rage because we are "At Home with God". We can rage because we know the reality of His presence with us. We can shout at God because even though we may not feel His presence with us now, we know that in the past we have, and we are hanging on to that fact and our faith with our fingernails.

So, these Psalms are there very much for us as we learn to live At Home with God. They are there to help us to see that it is OK to be upset because of what life has thrown at you. They are there to help us see that being a Christian doesn't take you away from the muck of this life and the things that can completely unsettle you, that you are not immune to pain and grief and things going wrong. But in these times our faith gives us something to hold on to even if at times this feels like we are climbing a very steep rock face and we only have a few small hooks and ropes to help us.

To be honest there have been lots of other times that I have used these words from the Psalms to help me in my life. I have at times, like most of us, not understood why certain things are happening or have happened. I have wondered why God has let them happen, I have raged at Him for not

---

[47] Psalm 13 NIV

intervening when someone I knew faced an untimely death, or a child, I had contact with, faced a life changing disability. These are the times when we often ask why, why did God not intervene, why did God let this happen?

However, in contrast when I faced a cancer diagnosis, I did not ask that question instead I answered it by saying why not me? You see I think that God gave me an acceptance of the fact that He doesn't cause these things to happen and when they do He is deeply saddened by them. If God loves us unconditionally then it goes without saying that He must be in pain when we are in pain. As His children He feels our pain just like we feel the pain of our own children. There have been times, even when they were in young adulthood, I have wanted to take away the pain that one of my children is going through. That seems to me to be a very natural reaction and often we hear parents say something like – "I just wish it was me lying there instead of them". God cares just like this, and just like I would wrap my children in my arms when they were small and needed to be reassured of my love, that is exactly what he wants to do with us. My children would wail and cry because they hurt, and my hug would somehow miraculously bring relief to them. It's the same when we rail at God and then let Him show us that we are not alone that He cares too and is there for us.

If we are genuinely "At Home with God" living out a relationship with Him, then we can rage and get cross and tell Him what's going on in our lives. He knows already but just like a close relationship with someone else our relationship with God means we can be real in how we are feeling and how we relate to Him. Being "At Home with God" is a place of safety to vent our feelings, to shout and scream, to rage and fume and yet to know that God is there with us and beside us and holding us in this time. He wants us to know His love and His presence.

Questions to reflect:

What times in your life have you felt like shouting and screaming at others about your situation? Did you try shouting and screaming at God?

---

*Home is safe, comfortable, a
warm feeling being surrounded by
family and pets, relaxing, recharge
batteries, Your own haven where you
aren't judged!*

Sharon, Dorset

Chapter 12

Home can be a place of healing

As we previously identified home can be a place of reality where emotions are expressed and held in a safe environment. Within this environment of safety and reality it can be a place of recovery, restoration, and ultimately a place of healing and wholeness. You don't get much more an idealised view of home life than the TV adverts for kitchens. In one, showing now, you see a small child falling outside, followed by her in the kitchen, sitting on an island with her legs in the sink, and the graze being gently swabbed by her father. An idealised view of home, but one, in some way, I am sure most of us can relate to. I doubt I am the only one who came home as a child with a nasty cut, graze, or bruise from slipping in the playground or falling of my bike. At home we will be put back together, if we can, by the gentle wipe of antiseptic, a dash of special cream and even a plaster to be proud of.

When I am physically exhausted by the pace of life then my home is healing. I take time out to rest and recuperate in what is famously called a duvet day. If I am struggling with an illness then my time at home can be healing as I wrap up warm, rest in my bed and drink lots of fluids.

If the relationships work well in our home, then it can be a place where we experience things which help us to heal physically and emotionally from the bashes and scrapes we get into in our daily life. Now of course I need to acknowledge that for many home has not been experienced as a place of healing. Home can be a place of trauma when relationships do not work, or the power dynamics are wrong. If that is the case for you, and the title of this chapter grates, I apologise. I hope also that what I say about the healing of being "At Home with God" will be helpful. I hope that the images I present will help you to imagine how being "At Home with God" may be a place of healing.

Often when we think about spiritual healing we think of the miraculous. It is easy to get into a debate about whether miracles happen today. In my own experience of praying for others I have witnessed miracles but also, I have experienced times when no healing is seen. There have been times when I have prayed for the healing of individuals that I have seen them healed of their illness physically, but at other times I have had to trust in an ultimate healing when people leave this earthly life to be with their God in heaven. This chapter is not going to cover healing in this way, as there have been many things written about this in other places. What I do want to speak of are a few simple ways that I can see being "At Home with God" can enable us to experience healing, and for this I want to draw on personal experience and what the Bible might say about this.

Home is where we can be wrapped up in love

There are times in my life even now when I want to be like a child and experience being wrapped in the arms of someone who loves me dearly. Isn't it healing to know that you are loved when you are hurting? It may be a physical pain, or it may be an emotional hurt, but the experience of being enfolded in love is one which can make everything seem so much better. We see this when a small child tumbles and is picked up and cuddled by the parent. The crying will stop even though the knee is still bruised and sore, and the pain hasn't gone away completely, but somehow the physical contact of the parent will make all seem so much better.

Jesus's earthly ministry was concentrated over a couple of years, and we see Him in this time not only teaching but carrying out many miracles. When we read the gospel accounts of Jesus' life you get a sense that physical healing was not his prime focus. However, we very often see His compassion for those in front of Him getting the better of Him and leading Him to perform a miracle. This is particularly clear from the healing of the Son of the Widow of Nain:

Soon afterwards, Jesus went to a town called Nain, and his disciples and a large crowd went along with him. [12] As he approached the town gate, a dead person was being carried out – the only son of his mother, and she was a widow. And a large crowd from the town was with her. [13] When the Lord saw her, his heart went out to her and he said, 'Don't cry.'

[14] Then he went up and touched the bier they were carrying him on, and the bearers stood still. He said, 'Young man, I say to you, get up!' [15] The dead man sat up and began to talk, and Jesus gave him back to his mother.[48]

We are not told a huge amount in this passage as to why particularly Jesus's heart went out to her, but original Greek description about the son gives us a clue. We know that he was a young man and that he had a particularly good relationship with his mother. The implication, therefore, is that the mother, a widow herself, would have been dependent upon her son for her own livelihood. The son's death was therefore not only huge in emotional terms for her, but also had enormous implications on her future. Jesus had compassion, He touched the bier and ordered the healing of the son who sat up and Jesus returns Him to his mother.

---

[48] Luke 7:11-15 NIV

This is a wonderful picture of compassion from Jesus. Throughout the gospel accounts of Jesus we see many more. But Jesus is not alone in speaking and showing love and compassion. The bible is littered with pictures of the love and compassion of God. Here are just two more examples to pause and reflect on.

Because of the Lord's great love we are not consumed, *for his compassions never fail.*[49] *but those who hope in the Lord will renew their strength. They will soar on wings like eagles; they will run and not grow weary, they will walk and not be faint.*[50]

I have certainly experienced the power of healing by knowing the presence of God when I was hurting both physically and emotionally. It feels very much like you are held in the arms of one who will not let you go and who understands exactly what you are going through. When I pray for those experiencing pain, I will pray that they will know the reality of being held in God's hands. That is indeed a prayer for healing as His presence brings peace and comfort.

Home is where we can know forgiveness

I knew one woman who was wracked in bitterness throughout her life. It stopped her enjoyment of what she had got in front of her, as she always went back to the hurt she had received from a past individual. This bitterness crippled her in forming relationships, and enjoying the life that she had been given, and the relationships that she had. Lack of forgiveness can lead to bitterness. The Ven Mila Smallman, a former Archdeacon in the Church of England, tragically lost both her daughters when they were murdered in a random

---

49 Lamentations 3:22 NIV
50 Isaiah 40:31 NIV

attack in London. Speaking of her feelings towards their murder she said these words:

"When we hold hatred for someone, it's not only them who is held captive, it's you, because your thoughts become consumed by revenge. I refuse to give him that power. He is a nonentity to me." [51]

These are emotional words but sum up the power of holding onto hatred and not moving forward with our emotions.

But lack of forgiveness also has a negative effect in the other way too. Feeling that we have not been forgiven can lead us to have detrimental feelings of failure and grief. When Jesus encountered people who needed healing you would have expected Him to say to them something like "be healed". Instead, time and time again He said to them "your sins are forgiven". Why? It could be interpreted that their sins had caused their illness or disability. This seems to me an interpretation that could lead us to unhelpful places, and I am not sure is right. What I think He was saying here was this, He was not only healing them physically, but He was putting right some of the emotional baggage that they carried too.

Just as at home with those we love we can learn to forgive and be forgiven, accepting God as part of our lives and living "At Home with Him" can allow this forgiveness to be healing and bring us wholeness. St Paul sums this up so well when he writing to the Ephesian Church says this:

Be kind to one another, tender-hearted, forgiving one another, as God in Christ forgave you. [52]

---

[51] Quoted in Church Times 7th July 2021
[52] Ephesians 4:32 NIV

Home is where we can be made whole

In years gone by if you had been seriously ill or had had surgery you would go to a convalescence home, possibly by the seaside, to recover. Those days are long gone, but still there is an expectation that you will take time off to recover from illness or surgery. This time that you spend at home is restorative. When I was about to have major surgery, a TV was installed in our bedroom so that when I came home I could relax and recuperate, and enjoy the delights or otherwise of day time TV without having to go very far. Home is very much a place where we become whole again.

In Jesus's day some illness separated people from those they loved as they were seen as characteristically unclean. We tend to think of leprosy here, but there is a wonderful account of Jesus healing a woman who had been bleeding for a number of years, and therefore was an outcast from her village community. We see her coming up to Jesus in the background and not wanting to make a fuss just touching His robe. As she touched Him, she was healed. But Jesus realised something had happened ,so gently asks her to make herself known. In this encounter with Jesus the woman is not only restored to health, but she is reinstated in her community – she is literally made whole again.[53]

There are times when I need to be made whole again particularly when I have experienced something that has hurt me greatly. I may need to forgive, but I also may need to be able to work out what to do with this hurt, and how to handle it. Our mental wellbeing can be a fragile thing and so often we need to go somewhere we can hand over the things on our hearts. We need to give ourselves space to work these though. The experience of mindfulness or reflection can help. But alongside this prayer and spiritual contemplation

---

53 Story found in Luke 8:43-48

can have a big part to play in our healing and restoring us to wholeness. Often it is only through supernatural help that we can come to a place of acceptance of what has happened to us, of learning to give and receive forgiveness, and be able to move on in a new way.

In Japanese culture there is a process of art called Kintsugi. Here broken, or cracked areas of pottery, are mended, and restored using a lacquer mixed with gold. This method takes the broken pot and makes it even more beautiful, as where there were cracks, they now glisten with gold. I find this a helpful analogy to use when thinking about our lives and healing. We are all broken and cracked by the things that life throws at us. Our brokenness can be physical but often its emotional and psychological. But the capacity for healing allows our restoration and wholeness. In the restoration process of Kintsugi the pots become more beautiful, adorned with the beauty of gold shining through where there were imperfections or fractures. If being "At Home with God" is a place of healing, then we begin the journey to become even more beautiful. In healing our lives are restored in new ways, and the scars, from the journey, are now changed to be beautiful and display the healing power of our creator.

Questions to reflect on:

Are there areas of your life where being "At Home with God" could bring healing?

How might your life look portrayed as a Kintsugi pot?

*Home is my family around the table
eating a roast dinner.*

Lucy, Berkshire

Chapter 13

Home is where we sit round a table with friends and family

Living "At Home with God" is very much about the relationship between us and our creator. However, God then calls us to be part of His family, the Church, and develop relationships with others. As we near the end of this exploration of faith, I want to spend a little time now thinking about this, using the analogy of sitting around a table.

Some of my most vibrant memories of my home have been times sat round the table with friends and family. I consider myself a very hospitable person and really enjoy entertaining those I know and love by trying out new recipes. But the process of sitting round the table with others is so much more than what we put on the table, and what we eat. The process of sitting round the table is all about the conversation, the jokes that are shared and the pulling of legs, the news that is conveyed to each other and the emotion that this engenders. Sitting round the table is a fundamental part of our lives and is one which we all missed when it was taken away from us during Covid 19.

In our house we try very hard to sit at the table to eat together, rather than taking a tray in front of the TV, but I must admit there are some evenings when this is all I want to do. You will see so called experts on TV programs helping parents with so called problem children, or other experts trying to help families save money, installing the fundamentals of sitting down and eating together to help resolve some of the problems. So, sitting round the table is good for family life according to the experts.

But sitting round a table together can show families as they really are. I remember vividly the arrival of my sister-in-law to our family life at home and around the table. As the youngest of four children all very vocal, the conversation was loud and went on and on. Our table was a noisy affair and there was much competition to see who could add to the conversation. In contrast my sister-in-law came from a much quieter family and later admitted that she had to go home to lie down and take pain killers after a visit for Sunday lunch. I remembered this when I was to introduce my future husband to the family and did it in smaller doses. My family life was certainly loud and full of laughter, teasing and emotion and often all of these were displayed around the dinner table.

Making yourself "At Home with God" is about the offer to sit around a table. This table is made by a carpenter from Nazareth, who lived an extraordinary life. The table is unusual because it stretches on and on and will squeeze in an indefinite number of people. This table is open to all, it's a place of hospitality, of refreshment. You may sit at this table with some rather odd people because the invitation to sit is open to all, no matter who you are or where you come from.

The invitation to sit at this table comes from the carpenter Himself, the carpenter of Nazareth, Jesus. The invitation to eat with Him and others comes throughout the gospels as we see so many different accounts of Jesus eating with others. But there are various things that are distinctly different about this table than most tables we sit around with others.

There's no hierarchy

When I was at boarding school in our dining hall, we had a top table. Those who were in the top of the school and either prefects or head of house would sit there along with the staff from our house. The hierarchy was clear, the rest of us would sit below them literally as their table was on a high platform. But around the table of Jesus there is no hierarchy as evidenced by this encounter with the tax collector Levi.

[27] *After this, Jesus went out and saw a tax collector by the name of Levi sitting at his tax booth. "Follow me," Jesus said to him,* [28] *and Levi got up, left everything and followed him.*

[29] *Then Levi held a great banquet for Jesus at his house, and a large crowd of tax collectors and others were eating with them.* [30] *But the Pharisees and the teachers of the law who belonged to their sect complained to his disciples, "Why do you eat and drink with tax collectors and sinners?"*

[31] *Jesus answered them, "It is not the healthy who need a doctor, but the sick.* [32] *I have not come to call the righteous, but sinners to repentance."* [54]

I love the fact that Jesus turns the expectations of others on their heads. For the Pharisees they would certainly not have entertained the idea of sitting with those who they considered were not worthy of their presence. But Jesus just goes along and joins in the banquet.

The Pharisees would have said that you had to qualify in some way to sit at their table. Jesus just invites all to sit at his. Because of Jesus' unconditional love and acceptance you don't have to do or say anything to be welcome at this table you just have to show up. That's an amazing invitation from Him. But Jesus himself realised that for many people there

---

[54] Luke 5:27-32 NIV

would be reasons that they would not accept this invitation. Jesus spoke of this in yet another parable He told of a wedding banquet that was held:

[16] *Jesus replied: "A certain man was preparing a great banquet and invited many guests.* [17] *At the time of the banquet he sent his servant to tell those who had been invited, 'Come, for everything is now ready.'*

[18] *"But they all alike began to make excuses. The first said, 'I have just bought a field, and I must go and see it. Please excuse me.'*

[19] *"Another said, 'I have just bought five yoke of oxen, and I'm on my way to try them out. Please excuse me.'*

[20] *"Still another said, 'I just got married, so I can't come.'*

[21] *"The servant came back and reported this to his master. Then the owner of the house became angry and ordered his servant, 'Go out quickly into the streets and alleys of the town and bring in the poor, the crippled, the blind and the lame.'*

[22] *"'Sir,' the servant said, 'what you ordered has been done, but there is still room.'*

[23] *"Then the master told his servant, 'Go out to the roads and country lanes and compel them to come in, so that my house will be full.* [24] *I tell you, not one of those who were invited will get a taste of my banquet.'"*[55]

How those who gave their excuses missed out on the great party and what feeble excuses they used. But the hospitality of the man was radical. He opened up the invitation to those who wouldn't normally be expected to be invited, those on the edge of society. This parable explores the amazing hospitality of Jesus Himself, and His call for us to sit at His table without hierarchy.

---

[55] Luke 14:16-24 NIV

Sometimes we are served and sometimes we get up to do the serving

Often at the ordination of deacons in the Church of England the Bishop wraps a towel round their robes and stoops down to wash the feet of those who are to be ordained. It is a poignant reminder to those starting their journey of being a "Rev" that service is at the heart of their calling. It is an act that re-enacts an important part of the Jesus story.

The night before Jesus died, we know that He had supper with his disciples. The accounts of it are clear and they shared a Passover feast together. Before this we see in John's gospel an account of Jesus getting down and taking the role of a servant by washing his disciples' feet.

Washing feet is not the most pleasant thing to do it has to be said. The feet of the disciples would have been hot and dusty from their day and their walk to the house to share supper. Washing feet is also an intensely personal experience. And yet Jesus who was their leader and teacher gets down with a towel and a jug of water and washes their feet. It is an act of love and of service. And in it he is showing what it means to be His follower:

When he had finished washing their feet, he put on his clothes and returned to his place. "Do you understand what I have done for you?" he asked them. [13] "You call me 'Teacher' and 'Lord,' and rightly so, for that is what I am. [14] Now that I, your Lord and Teacher, have washed your feet, you also should wash one another's feet. [15] I have set you an example that you should do as I have done for you. [16] Very truly I tell you, no servant is greater than his master, nor is a messenger greater than the one who sent him. [17] Now that you know these things, you will be blessed if you do them.[156]

---

[56] John 13:12-17 NIV

Sometimes there are arguments and the table is thumped but always there is a call to make peace

I was always taught in polite conversation never to talk about politics, religion or sex. However, we know that at different times these controversial subjects can come out in conversation, sometimes with heated debate. During the Brexit debate I was at least once at a dinner table which got thumped. It was thumped by the one holding the minority view around it who was desperate to get his point across. Things can get heated in conversation as we discuss things that we are passionate about. I have also been around tables where the difference between two people becomes so obvious that you strongly suspect that their relationship, in the long term, is going to become untenable.

In contrast to relationships not working out, the table that Jesus calls us to sit round is a table that needs to come to peace. We can differ in views, but we must always seek to work towards reconciliation. After Jesus' resurrection we are told that He greeted his disciples three times with the words "*Peace be with you*". In the writings of St Paul to the various churches we see His call strongly for them to live in peace.

Finally, brothers and sisters, rejoice! Strive for full restoration, encourage one another, be of one mind, live in peace. And the God of love and peace will be with you.[57]

What is this table?

So what is this table that we are talking of here? Well simply the table is Jesus' table and is full of those who want to follow Him and those who are discovering what it is all about. When Jesus went back to heaven after his resurrection, His disciples were sent out in the power of the Holy Spirit to tell others about Him, and to invite others to join in the Jesus

---

[57] 2 Corinthians 11:4 NIV

movement. They began to share life together, both in each other's homes or in the synagogue. They would have a meal together and sharing bread and wine they would remember Jesus' death. The acts of the apostles in the Bible shows how this movement of Jesus' followers quickly establishes groups or churches spreading out from Jerusalem and into the Mediterranean.

So, this was the start of what we now would refer to as Church. Over the years people have expressed this in different ways and fallen out with each other and formed their own particular group or denomination. But in its purity, the Church is a group of individuals who want to begin to sit at Jesus' table and learn from each other, to seek to follow in His way by serving each other and by living His Kingdom values in the world.

A few years ago, I took a group from the Church I was working in away for the weekend. We had fun spending time with each other, getting to know each other a little better, and having some teaching from a well-known speaker. At the end of the weekend I was looking around the group and noticed that the age span of this group ranged from 8 to 80. This struck me as significant because I couldn't think of another gathering of people that would span this sort of age range except a family. At present in my extended family the youngest is under a year old and her great grandma is 88.

In a sense Church can be described as a family too. Most of those who are part of it will see themselves as in relationship with each other because they share the same faith. Those who are not yet part of it will be welcomed to explore, and to join in with the family gathering, as if they were invited to be part of a meal around a table. And in this family, around this table, there is no hierarchy, we are all called to serve and yet to be served and we aim to live in peace with each other.

That's a lovely description but to be truly honest like most families there are times when it doesn't quite look like that. That's the problem of all being human with our own preferences and peculiarities. But like us all as individuals, Church is always a work in progress, and the table is open to all to be part of, even if occasionally you don't get on with the person sitting next to you.

The analogy of the table continues through when we think about sharing a meal together as this is a central part of the life of the Community of faith – the Church. The meal, which is known variously as Holy Communion, the Mass, the Eucharist, consists of bread and wine and remembers the final meal of Jesus and his disciples before his crucifixion.

19 And he took bread, gave thanks and broke it, and gave it to them, saying, "This is my body given for you; do this in remembrance of me."

20 In the same way, after the supper he took the cup, saying, "This cup is the new covenant in my blood, which is poured out for you.58

In this account from Luke's gospel we see Jesus say the words "Do this in remembrance of me". So the act of taking bread and wine remembers the fact that Jesus died for us on the cross to make us at one with God again. This simple meal, that may be shared in different ways by different groups of Christians, fundamentally is a meal of remembrance. In sharing this meal, of bread and wine, we remember the amazing love of God and Jesus' sacrifice on the cross.

As an ordained minister in the Church of England I cannot do have my own private communion service of bread and wine. I am not allowed to do this because the sharing of

---

58 Luke 22:19-20 NIV

the meal is vitally important. Why? Because the act of being together is part of the remembering. By being together we are reminded that it's not just about us but that we are part of something bigger. The table we sit at is Jesus' table, open to all and that we are part of the worldwide group of people who call themselves followers of Jesus. That this table is vast and long and encompasses all and that all are welcome to come and share this meal and eat at this table, at home with God.

Questions to reflect on:

How does the image of the table resonate with you?

Why do you think it is helpful for Christians to re-enact the last supper in this way

Home can be anywhere, It's what you carry in your heart. Not things or belongings or bricks and mortar.

Ann, Dorset

Chapter 14

Home for Eternity

To end this book, I want us to move our thinking from here on earth to a life beyond. I think many people would see being "At Home with God" primarily in these terms. As a Christian the concept of a heavenly home is deeply important to me. However, I hope you will have grasped throughout this book the importance I place of living "At Home with God" on this earth. That living in this way gives life and meaning to our lives now, whilst also holding the hope of eternity. But I end with this chapter to think towards life beyond earth and the hope of continuing our life with God into a new place.

There have been times of my lives when I have experienced a thin place, when earth seems close to heaven, and it is possible to grasp what it might be like to be in the heavenly realms. This has been in different places including special church buildings, out in nature or being with someone as they have approached death itself. These intensely spiritual moments have helped me to trust in a more profound way that there is something more that we are promised, and eternity, "At Home with God", starts on earth but continues beyond.

Jesus said these words which speak clearly of this. They are recorded by John in his gospel, and as words of hope for eternity are often used at funerals

"Do not let your hearts be troubled. You believe in God[a]; believe also in me. ² My Father's house has many rooms; if that were not so, would I have told you that I am going there to prepare a place for you? ³ And if I go and prepare a place for you, I will come back and take you to be with me that you also may be where I am. ⁴ You know the way to the place where I am going."

⁵ Thomas said to him, "Lord, we don't know where you are going, so how can we know the way?"

⁶ Jesus answered, "I am the way and the truth and the life. No one comes to the Father except through me. ⁷ If you really know me, you will know[b] my Father as well. From now on, you do know him and have seen him."⁵⁹

In the days of Jesus, in a traditional Nazareth village, the homes would have been simple, consisting of a couple of rooms around the central courtyard. When a son in the family married a new room would be added to the home for the new couple to be apart, but also part of the family unit. When Jesus says these words he is saying that God is adding a new room for each of us in his Father's house. It is a house that just keeps on growing and growing.

But as well as talking about adding a room Jesus here says that the way to be part of this home is by trusting and following him. He says this because at this point He knew the path that He was to take to the cross and resurrection to show his defeat of both sin and death.

Jesus hung on the cross between two criminals. One mocked Him but the other realised that this man Jesus was different:

One of the criminals who hung there hurled insults at him: "Aren't you the Messiah? Save yourself and us!"

---

⁵⁹ John 14:1-6 NIV

⁴⁰ But the other criminal rebuked him. "Don't you fear God," he said, "since you are under the same sentence? ⁴¹ We are punished justly, for we are getting what our deeds deserve. But this man has done nothing wrong."

⁴² Then he said, "Jesus, remember me when you come into your kingdom.[a]"

⁴³ Jesus answered him, "Truly I tell you, today you will be with me in paradise."⁶⁰

Jesus' words to the thief speak of a resurrection after death to a new life in "paradise" or eternity as we think of it. It's a promise He alluded to in different ways throughout His life but here at this point of death we see the hope clearly.

But what does this place of home look like? Most portrayals we see would show lots of fluffy clouds and angels dressed in white with possibly tinsel halos. Often people have said to me words like "heaven sounds a bit boring, I think I'll risk the alternative." I guess if we have the impression of God being a bit of a kill joy, not allowing anything good to happen, that might be the case, or indeed if we just see heaven as a massive church service, I certainly hope that it won't be! But I have to say I think the Bible makes it clear that this is not the case.

The Old Testament in the Bible seems to suggest that heaven is going to be when the garden of Eden is restored. So, earth will be just like it was when God created it, and therefore it will be full of amazing things and the created world will be restored from the pain and suffering that has gripped it. The main book in the Bible which talks about the end times and visualises heaven for us is the book of Revelation, the visions of St John. Here he speaks of heaven as the new Jerusalem, the place where God will dwell. He

---

⁶⁰ Luke 23:39-43 NIV

envisages a river running through it which is a river of life and there is a tree of life which holds leaves which will be for the healing of the nations. The overall impression therefore is that heaven is a place where God dwells and all the things which have caused pain on earth have gone.

Then I saw "a new heaven and a new earth,"[a] for the first heaven and the first earth had passed away, and there was no longer any sea. ² I saw the Holy City, the new Jerusalem, coming down out of heaven from God, prepared as a bride beautifully dressed for her husband. ³ And I heard a loud voice from the throne saying, "Look! God's dwelling place is now among the people, and he will dwell with them. They will be his people, and God himself will be with them and be their God. ⁴ 'He will wipe every tear from their eyes. There will be no more death'[b] or mourning or crying or pain, for the old order of things has passed away."

⁵ He who was seated on the throne said, "I am making everything new!" Then he said, "Write this down, for these words are trustworthy and true."

⁶ He said to me: "It is done. I am the Alpha and the Omega, the Beginning and the End. To the thirsty I will give water without cost from the spring of the water of life. ⁷ Those who are victorious will inherit all this, and I will be their God and they will be my children[61].

A place where God dwells is key to our understanding of what this may be like. You see in God we see only good things. We know that He is love itself, love is the heart of His character it can't be taken away from him. We know also that He is the light that shines in the dark place. This love and light will be what we experience. We are not sure what it will be like, or how it will look, but we know that what we will

---

[61] Revelation 21:1-7 NIV

experience is the intensity of both love and light. This seems to me to be far from boring.

In the Chronicles of Narnia CS Lewis begins to imagine heaven. The children have been backwards and forwards into Narnia through the wardrobe. They have experienced good, but also they have experienced intense evil. As they come to the end of their time in Narnia, they are part of the final battle of good and evil and move to a different sort of Narnia:

It is hard to explain how this sunlit land was different from the old Narnia as it would be to tell you how the fruits of that country taste....... The new one was a deeper country: every rock and flower and blade of grass looked as if it meant more. I can't describe it any better than that: if ever you get there you will know what I mean[62]

What speaks to me here was the intensity with which they are experiencing what is like the old but is somehow new. I think this is a helpful analogy for us. The new heaven and earth that John writes of in Revelation is just that, it is a restored pace, made perfect and governed by the light and love of God Himself and in the words of CS Lewis this is the beginning of a new story:

But for them it was only the beginning of the real story. All their life in this world and all their adventures in Narnia had only been the cover and the title page: now at last they were beginning Chapter One of the Great Story which no one on earth has read: which goes on for ever: in which every chapter is better than the one before.[63]

This is the wonderful hope that is right at the centre of the Christian faith. We live "At Home with God" and experience His presence, His peace, His joy, His healing in this life. We can do this by spending time with Him and with others who

---

[62] Lewis . C.S. (1998) *The Last Battle*, Colour Edition, Collins, London pg 179-80
[63] Lewis . C.S. (1998) *The Last Battle*, Colour Edition, Collins, London pg 192

share this faith. And yet we wait for a new story to begin at the end of our earthly life. A story where somehow this life has only been a prequel, the next seems to be the real deal.

When my Dad was told that he had a recurrence of cancer and it was likely to be terminal, his response was incredible and taught me so much about faith and hope. Having been an airline pilot in both the RAF and British Airways he knew all about preparing for landing. For him, he likened his preparation at this point to doing the same, he had to get the right bits ready in the cockpit and certainly ensure that the wheels were going to go down properly. He said this because he knew that he was in the process of moving from the prequel to the real deal. My Dad indeed knew that he was truly going home, and it gives me joy in pain, with certainty, to be able to say that he is "At Home with God" in eternity.

The call to live "At Home with God" is one which starts in this life and follows through for eternity. I hope and pray that you have been able to journey with me through these pages, and that you might have begun to explore more of the amazing life that God offers when we make our home with Him. It has been a pleasure and a privilege to explore these themes and use this analogy to describe not only my relationship with God, but how He has brought change and transformation to myself and others around me. I continue to pray that as you reflect on these words that you would be able to realise something of the magnitude of God's love for yourself, and take up His invitation to make Himself at home with you. Ultimately, I long for others to be able to say for certainty, now and for eternity, – I am truly "At Home with God".

Lucy Holt

Lucy has been leading St James Church in Poole since 2013. Her many roles in the Parish include being Chaplain to Poole RNLI lifeboat and a trustee of the Charity for the Homeless - Routes to Roots. Alongside this Lucy is a non-residentiary Canon of Salisbury Cathedral and Rural Dean of Poole and North Bournemouth. Prior to being in Poole Lucy was Vicar just outside Windsor and curate in North Buckinghamshire.

Prior to ordination Lucy had a career in the Health Service as a Registered Nurse and then a Health Visitor. She developed her academic interest in psychology by studying with the Open University whilst juggling the demands of small children.

In her spare time Lucy enjoys sea swimming, entering the water throughout the year without a wet suit. Lucy is a keen cook and baker, as well as occasionally picking up a paint brush to explore the mediums of both watercolour and acrylic paint.

Lucy is married to Andrew and they have two grown up daughters.